GOOSE
SHOOTING

GOOSE SHOOTING

Alasdair Mitchell

SWAN·HILL
PRESS

First published in the UK in 1997
by Swan Hill Press, an imprint of Airlife Publishing Ltd

British Library Cataloguing-in-Publication Data
  A catalogue record for this book
  is available from the British Library

ISBN 1 85310 793 X

Typeset by Servis Filmsetting Ltd, Manchester
Printed in England by St Edmundsbury Press, Bury St Edmunds, Suffolk.

Swan Hill Press

an imprint of Airlife Publishing Ltd.
101 Longden Road, Shrewsbury, SY3 9EB, England

Contents

Acknowledgements

I would like to thank the British Association for Shooting and Conservation (BASC) for their help in answering my queries. I must also thank the Wildfowl and Wetlands Trust (WWT), especially Carl Mitchell – a considerable authority on geese – who was kind enough to read through the chapter on the natural history of geese and made a number of helpful comments and clarifications. I strongly urge every wildfowler to join both the BASC and the WWT.

Thanks are also due to a number of goose guides who have become friends over the years. Chief among these is Percy Betts. Big-bore gunmaker and goose enthusiast Alan Myers also deserves a special mention, not least for imparting some of his knowledge of goose-shooting tactics. Some of my earliest goose flights were arranged by Alan Murray, a guide who has a real regard for geese. Martyn Howard, a fellow goose-shooting enthusiast, kindly allowed me to tell the tale of his debut with the Myers double four-bore, while my long-standing wildfowling companion Martin Selby-Lowndes has had little choice but to feature. I must also thank Dave Leeming, of the Ballistics Group at the Royal Military College of Science, Shrivenham, for his assistance with the chapter on shot sizes and loads.

I wish to thank the following publishers or copyright holders for giving me permission to reproduce items from various publications:

John Gregson, Editor of *Shooting Times and Country Magazine*, for articles of mine which were originally published in that magazine
A & C Black Ltd, for extracts from *The Practical Wildfowler*, by John Marchington
B T Batsford Ltd, for an extract from *Wild Geese of the World*, by Myrfyn Owen
Hodder Headline Ltd, for extracts from *The Eye of the Wind*, by Sir Peter Scott
Lyons & Burford (USA) for extracts from *The Wildfowler's Quest*, by George Reiger
The Editor of *Wildfowl* (the WWT's journal) for an extract from *Observations On The Pinkfooted Goose In Central Iceland*, by D E Hardy
Faber & Faber Ltd, for extracts from *And Clouds Flying*, by Ian Pitman
Colin Willock, for an extract from *Kenzie The Wild-Goose Man*
Angela Watkins-Pitchford, for extracts from *Tide's Ending*, by 'BB' and also for some of his scraperboard illustrations
The Crowood Press Ltd, for extracts from *Fowling For Duck*, by Mike Swan
Tideline Publishing Company Ltd, for an extract from *Tales of a Wildfowler*, by Arthur Cadman
Geoffrey Bles Ltd, for extracts from *Norfolk Fowler*, by Alan Savory

Preface

It all began with a book.

Idling in the school library one rainy afternoon, I found a hardback book entitled *Tide's Ending*, by the enigmatic 'BB'. I recognised the author, because he had also written an award-winning children's book called *The Little Grey Men*, which my father had given me some years before. He had explained that BB was actually Denys Watkins-Pitchford, but even Father did not understand the significance of those two letters. It was some years before I realised that BB was the traditional shot size for geese. I opened *Tide's Ending* and began to read.

Within a few pages I found myself transported to an untamed land of saltmarsh and sandbanks, where great grey geese battled across the stormy sky in ragged formation, their wild calls thrilling the hardy gunner crouching in a creek with his fowling piece. It was a tale of adventure and mystery, imbued with the true hunter's respect for his quarry. Best of all, it was not set in some faraway, inaccessible place like Africa, but here, in Britain. Until I read *Tide's Ending*, I had never even thought about what lay beyond the sea wall; I had no idea that it marked the boundary of the last real wilderness in Britain. There and then I decided that wildfowling – as opposed to shooting – was for me. And at the pinnacle of the wildfowler's quarry list was the wild goose, epitomising the wild, restless spirit of the sport.

The only slight drawback was that I did not have a gun, and lived in the very centre of England – just about as far from the coast as it is possible to get. Fortunately, I had a kindred spirit at school called Martin Selby-Lowndes. His father owned a couple of rather antique shotguns and knew how to use them. Moreover, he had permission to shoot on some nearby land. Having sorted out the formalities, including being drilled in all matters concerning safety, Martin and I duly sallied forth in search of fowl.

Our main area of operations was a couple of hundred acres of rather uninspiring farmland on the edge of what was in the process of becoming the new town of Milton Keynes. There was a scraggy elm spinney, a few hedges, some old pasture bristling with thistles and, of major importance, a stretch of the infant River Ouse. It was not the Solway or the Wash, but it did us very well in those early days. There were snipe, partridges and duck to shoot. The unkempt hedges were full of songbirds and insects, the elms were thick with rooks, and the weed-choked river bulged with fish and amphibians.

We bought waders, balaclavas and thornproof jackets, and stumped about the place at what we called 'evening flight', bagging an occasional unlucky mallard. We looked for every opportunity to get out with a gun, particularly savouring the all too rare spells of severe weather; somehow, a duck shot in a blizzard seemed more in keeping with the spirit of the sport, and we relished the test of our hardiness.

Meanwhile, the pylons and scaffolding of a burgeoning Milton Keynes loomed ever nearer, advancing hundreds of yards in a few short summer months before being held in check by the mud of winter – rather like an invading army, which is exactly how we viewed the bulldozers and their helmeted drivers.

We had one final, glorious episode before 'they' finally won. They had dredged out a section of the river and scraped the topsoil from a few nearby acres in preparation for an 'amenity lake'. After a period of intense frost, which froze the bare ground into an impermeable surface like rough concrete, a series of Atlantic fronts swept across the country, bringing torrential rain.

We tried to imagine the effects of the freak conditions as we travelled to our familiar ground before dawn on the third day of the storm. On arrival, the scene was unrecognisable. Through the stormy darkness we were dimly aware of the dull, pewter gleam of vast sheets of water. At times, the rain on my hood sounded – and felt – like handfuls of coarse sand being dashed against the fabric. If we could not get to the Wash, the Wash had come to us – or so it seemed.

8

And there were duck – hundreds of them, more than we had ever seen before: teal, mallard, even wigeon, a traditional coastal wildfowler's quarry whose wild, whistling calls we had only ever read about before.

As the light increased, it became increasingly difficult to hide in the suddenly bleak landscape. We had made a record bag of five mallard and a teal when two more mallard appeared, heading straight for us. There was nowhere to hide. We were at the edge of the river, but what remained of the bank crumbled even as we watched, eaten away by the voracious brown torrent. There was nothing for it but to fling ourselves flat on the ground, in what we presumed was the proper style for disciples of BB.

The duck came on into the gale. We could see their bills opening and closing as they called, though the sound was snatched away by the wind. Icy water seeped between the layers of our clothing.

They were in range. One of us shouted to the other, without looking round: 'You take the one on the right, I'll take the one on the left – go!' With that we both sprang to our knees, cascading water, and fired almost simultaneously. The detonations were reduced to mere pops by the wind. As if perfectly synchronised, each duck instantly folded into a rag-like jumble of wings, and fell flailing toward the sodden surface.

Yet if this feat marked a high note, it also signalled the beginning of the end. In later years, I was to remember that once we lose a shooting ground, we never get it back (not in this lifetime, anyway).

Walking along the dull, neat banks of the newly-canalised river one foggy day during the last autumn we had there, I made some sort of vaguely derogatory comment about the state of the old place. Martin took offence on the grounds that I was being disloyal to the land which had given us such sport. As a result, we plodded along in hostile silence.

Suddenly, there was a distant goose call. We froze. Neither of us had actually heard a wild goose before, but we instinctively recognised the call when we heard it. For one thing, it was not unlike the noises we had heard farmyard geese make, although it seemed to have an ethereal quality about it, being broadcast from the misty sky.

More calls followed, coming closer. Then, out of the fog, they materialised – five great greylags, flying just 20 yards off the ground, clawing through the damp atmosphere on wings which spanned more than 5 feet. Their lavender-grey forewings lit up as they crossed a shaft of weak sunlight, making them look almost exotic.

As it happened, we were a hundred yards off to one side, so we could not shoot. I am not sure that we would have fired in any case. We just gazed, dumbstruck, as the almost mythical birds flew on and disappeared into the fog again. They were probably only feral stock, but that was not the point. Martin was triumphant.

A few weeks later, we went into a nearby information centre, a cedar-shingled building of almost antiseptic cleanliness which, from the outside, seemed more suited to Finland than north Buckinghamshire. The inside was festooned with leaflets, posters and static displays exhorting us to use the plethora of state-sponsored outdoor activities available in the area.

We were after a large-scale map on which we intended to plot likely flight lines (it was becoming difficult to keep up with all the new 'water features').

With what in retrospect seems like awesome naivety, we went to the counter and enquired. A woman dressed like an airline stewardess gave us a synthetic smile and reached into a filing cabinet. She asked us why we wanted the map. We told her. Blank looks. We explained. Blank looks gave way to dawning comprehension, then hostile incredulity. The cabinet clanged shut.

We shuffled out in our muddy thornproofs and emerged, blinking, into the harsh urban sunlight. For the first time, we noticed the roar of cars on the new dual carriageway. Time had moved on, and left us behind.

I drove past the old place recently. With its carefully mown grass, picnic sites and jogging tracks, it looked like something from a holiday camp brochure. The local authority had stocked the bleak lake with coarse fish, and several fishermen were hunched over long rods. Thus the modern urbanite is permitted to indulge his natural hunting instinct. Brightly coloured dinghies and windsurfers swept and swooped contemptuously among the fishermen's floats.

Over-fed tame duck squabbled around an overflowing litter bin. Incredibly, there were also geese – albeit only Canadas. But their presence lifted my spirits. Seeing them reminded me of a passage in T H White's *England Have My Bones*: 'When London bridge has tumbled down, and the sewers of the hive have ceased to pollute the waters, there will be salmon opposite the Imperial Chemicals building, but no Imperial Chemicals building opposite the salmon'.

This was written in 1934. In the 1980s, salmon returned to the Thames, and duly swam upstream past the ICI building. As for the building, it was still there last time I looked. But time will tell.

CHAPTER ONE

The Call of the Wild Goose

There've been times when it's been snowing and blowing that I've been
singing at the top of my voice because I knew no one else was up and no one
could hear me. I've thoroughly enjoyed every moment of it, and if I had my
time to come I'd do it all again, just the same. Just exactly the same.

Kenzie Thorpe, wildfowling guide
(Kenzie the Wild-goose Man by Colin Willock)

nthusiasm, it seems to me, is generally infectious – or perhaps we
goose shooters are just naturally susceptible to it. Perhaps this is why
I can understand the gentle fanaticism of the carp fisher even if I do
not share his devotion to carp. The common bond between us is a fascination with a particularly noble quarry, combined with age-old hunting
instincts.

One of the most positive aspects of shooting and fishing is the way in
which they bind one into the rhythms of the natural world. The trout fisherman delights in a warm June evening, while the coastal wildfowler prays for
a tearing blizzard in January. The jaded urbanite, on the other hand, takes
his cue from the simpering TV weather forecasters, who seem to think that
anything other than unseasonable warmth and fatuous blue skies deserves
an apology.

Trying to explain the appeal of wildfowling is a difficult task. Even those on the fringes of the faith, such as roughshooters, have difficulty in accepting that one wild duck, bagged in a sporting manner in its own wild environment, is worth five pheasants. As for a wild goose – well, a wild goose is to a reared pheasant what a fresh-run spring salmon is to a pellet-stuffed stewpond trout.

There are those who draw a clear line between 'proper' wildfowling, by which they mean coastal wildfowling, and the pursuit of wildfowl inland. I have some sympathy with these foreshore purists but, in the final analysis, the distinctive feature of wildfowling is the wildfowl. Nobody would classify the shooting of hand-reared mallard as wildfowling, but I maintain that the key factor here is the origin and nature of the quarry. You cannot get anything wilder than a wild goose. Most geese are shot inland today, and this has much to do with the fact that most geese now spend most of their time inland. Where the quarry goes, the hunter follows. There is nothing intrinsically second-rate about inland goose shooting.

The sport of goose shooting involves the pursuit of geese in a restrained and sporting manner with a shotgun. As a wildfowling quarry, the wild goose is the ultimate prize. Very few coastal wildfowlers dedicate themselves solely to the pursuit of geese, for sound practical reasons, but inland the situation is rather different, with a whole section of commerce having grown up to service the requirements of the specialist goose shooter.

In some isolated cases, this has led to excessive bags and unsporting behaviour. A few extreme examples have caused genuine outrage, but a crackdown by responsible goose shooters has ensured that the unsavoury activities of the greedy few have been curtailed.

Goose shooting grew out of traditional wildfowling in much the same way as pigeon shooting, with all its attendant theory and practice of decoying, grew out of general roughshooting. In order to trace the evolution of modern goose shooting, we have to identify the particular features of wildfowling. This in turn entails a brief look at the history of the sport.

Wildfowling is perhaps the most elemental of field sports. In essence, it has changed little over the past 200 or so years; we still pursue the same wildfowl in the same wild places as our ancestors did, often using tactics and equipment that they would recognise. The key to successful wildfowling remains the ability to get within range of the quarry. This critical distance – a maximum of about 50 yards for a shoulder gun – has not really changed since the first ragged fowler tramped the marsh with a flintlock, despite the advent of modern propellants and weapons.

The first wildfowlers hunted for the pot and used every means available to them, including nets, spears and traps. In that age, the pursuit of geese and ducks was little more than a desperate and uncertain way to support a wretched life in a harsh world, where men's survival – and that of their families – depended on their prowess and luck in harvesting natural bounty. They did not choose to hunt wildfowl – they had to, in the same way that they had to kill other beasts and gather or tend edible plants. They did not have the luxury of treating wildfowling as a sport, and certainly had no inkling of sporting ethics as we would recognise them today. The name of the game was survival – pure, simple and brutal.

Conservation was an abstract concept, something which happened by default rather than design. Naturally, these subsistence hunters were very efficient in their use of the wildfowl they killed; little was wasted. And they probably had a certain respect for these wild and wary birds, perhaps believing that they had spirits too. But the only factors limiting their killing of wildfowl was their ability and opportunity to do so. Not that this really mattered in conservation terms, so long as the harvest was modest. But make no mistake: if they could have killed more wildfowl, then by instinct they would have done so without a qualm. Yet who are we to judge another culture by our own values?

If you believe that indigenous hunter-gatherer communities invariably show restraint during times of plenty, then a passage from George Reiger's book, *The Wildfowler's Quest*, might disabuse you. The American describes how he spent some time with a party of Inuit hunters in the Canadian Arctic. He witnessed them ambushing a nesting colony of snow geese, wiping out young and old alike with rifles and tent poles. None were spared. Reiger writes: 'I don't know how many dozen birds were killed, but I do know that when we slowly motored away from the shore, I looked back to an eerily empty valley that had been teeming with wildfowl only an hour before'.

Reiger thought that the hunt was over, but on the way back the Inuit came across a family party of five caribou. Once again, all the beasts were slaughtered. But the real horror was yet to come. On returning to their boats, the Inuit simply threw out all the dead snow geese to make room for the more highly prized caribou meat. 'The entire colony of greater snow geese went drifting into the dusk. On the run downriver, we passed their ghostly bodies wedged between rocks and stranded on gravel bars,' says Reiger.

Of course, these particular Inuit had modern weapons, which gave them a capability out of all proportion to that of their forebears. They behaved like a fox let loose in a chicken run. In the same way, the professional market gunners who eventually evolved out of the subsistence wildfowlers here in Britain saw little need for restraint. Their reasoning was straightforward: they lived off the proceeds of their skill in killing fowl, which they did by every means possible. As the nineteenth century dawned, however, some of these professionals began to adapt to changing circumstances, supplementing their meagre incomes by guiding a new breed of gentleman-gunner. These gentlemen were the first sporting wildfowlers, and their numbers increased steadily as the Victorian era blossomed. Wildfowling, with its connotations of hard exercise, delight in tackling adverse conditions and rigid self-denial, was particularly well matched to the mood of an age in which the British Empire held sway. People like Colonel Peter Hawker, Henry Folkard, Abel Chapman, John Guille Millais and Sir Ralph Payne-Gallwey epitomised this hardy breed. Soldiers, lawyers, landowners – they were hardly representative of the ordinary people, but it was for this very reason that wildfowling became bound by sporting ethics. Some were also considerable naturalists and ornithologists. Both Millais and Chapman were Fellows of the Zoological Society, and Chapman went on to found what became Kruger National Park in South Africa.

Many of these gentlemen-gunners came to regard punt gunning as the ultimate form of wildfowling, as certain die-hards do to this day. At the opposite end of the comfort scale, purpose-built fowling yachts equipped with swivel-guns roamed the estuaries. Yet shoulder guns retained their popularity, and if anything the sport became more accessible as manufacturing technology and mass transport improved. Anyone with a healthy constitution and an eagerness to brave wind and rain could wander the foreshore with a gun in search of fowl. By the standards of the time, class distinctions counted for little below the sea wall, and so it has remained.

By the end of the nineteenth century, coastal wildfowling was well established as a sport, with its own traditions and informal conventions. Between the two world wars it became even more popular, and the great marshes of the Solway, East Anglia and the Wash, in particular, became places of pilgrimage for a new breed of young, mobile, articulate, middle-class fowlers who had the means and the inclination to write about their sport.

One of these was James Wentworth Day. A journalist by profession, his enthusiasm for wildfowling seems to have been rooted in the marsh itself. In *The Modern Fowler,* published in 1934, he describes the land bordering the Wash in these stirring terms:

> I think if one were to live in this wide and open country of great fields and
> great seascapes, where the horizons are as wide as the sea itself, where the wind
> sweeps and roars, where the snows come straight from the Arctic, and the geese
> last saw land beneath the Midnight Sun, one might walk like a hero, live like
> a fighting-cock and die at a hundred.

Sir Peter Scott, the conservationist and founder of what became today's Wildfowl and Wetlands Trust (WWT), was an avid wildfowler in his early days, starting as an undergraduate at Cambridge. His first book, *Morning*

Flight, was published in 1935 and set the scene for a host of books which did much to popularise the sport. Unlike many earlier authors, Scott largely avoided giving instruction, but concentrated instead on conveying the emotional and aesthetic aspects of wildfowling. To this end, *Morning Flight* contained many of his now-famous paintings of wildfowl.

More recently, artists like Julian Novorol have continued the tradition of creating paintings which raise the hairs on the back of the neck of wildfowler and birdwatcher alike.

Wildfowling has spawned a prolific number of books, including some of a quality unmatched by any other branch of shooting. The literature of wildfowling has been a constant source of nourishment for the sport, enthusing each new generation in turn. The lure of escapism should not be underestimated. The very first sentence of Ian Pitman's *And Clouds Flying* sets the scene: 'To write, and in writing lose war and death and tedium of life in memories of starlit nights, of marram grass and grey saltings, of curlew and plover and duck, and of the whistle of wings cutting through cold winter air'. The poignancy sharpens when you realise that he wrote the book (which was subsequently illustrated by Peter Scott) while incarcerated in a German prisoner-of-war camp.

In broad terms, wildfowling books tend to fall into two categories: instructional works and those which are more descriptive, often based on anecdotes. As an example of the latter, BB's *Tide's Ending*, published in 1950, is a paragon. Originally an art master at Rugby School, he became a prolific author and columnist, writing on a wide variety of subjects, mostly with a countryside or natural history theme. BB was also a highly talented artist who illustrated both his own and many other books, always signing his pictures in his real name. He wrote several books about wildfowling and geese, but *Tide's Ending* was perhaps his best, with its unrivalled combination of atmospheric prose and evocative scraperboard etchings.

It was BB and writers like him who gently set out the ethics and conventions of the sport. They disdained large bags of geese, making it clear that the quarry was to be respected at all times, dead or alive. Nothing that was bagged was to be wasted. This precluded firing at fowl resting on ice, from where you might not be able to retrieve them. Out of range shooting, which might only prick birds, was frowned upon. The worst crime of all was to shoot at the geese out on the sands where they roosted, because it destroyed their sanctuary and would eventually drive them away.

Reading the wildfowling classics of the day, one can occasionally catch a glimpse of the world beyond the marsh – and what a cosy world it seems! Of course memory tends to be selective – we remember all the good things and forget the bad experiences. *Tide's Ending,* which presumably drew upon BB's experiences of the 1930s and 1940s, describes a world where trains ran on time, and to every nook and cranny of the British Isles, and where stationmasters were large, benevolent beings equipped with fob watches and immaculate gardens. The fowler would cycle from the station through the little village to his 'digs' at the pub. The kindly landlady would have cut out the tidetable from the local paper and propped it up on the chimney piece of the homely room where he would examine it by the flickering light of the fire as he drank his cocoa from a large enamelled mug.

It was an age of telegrams and tweed, hobnails and steam trains; an age where everybody was honest until proved otherwise. In *Fowler's Moon*, published in 1955, Nigel Thorneycroft matter-of-factly tells how he wrote off in response to a private advertisement and had a gun sent by ordinary post 'on approval'! If you found a flock of geese feeding inland, you sought the farmer and asked his permission. He would probably be happy to give it, and you might remember him with a bottle of whisky at Christmas if all had gone well. You might in fact be the only shooter he had seen that year.

The weather seems to have been 'better' in those days, too. Gales and tempests were apparently commonplace, as were intense frosts and heavy falls of snow. Time and again our heroes got to grips with their noble quarry only after enduring terrible hardships. They thought nothing of spending the stormy night shivering in a haystack (they had proper haystacks then) before plodding across dark and dangerous ooze to a favourite creek, always mindful of the treacherous tide which might cut them off.

Of course, this is all part of the mythology of wildfowling. It was never really quite like that, as we shall see in a later chapter. But it makes for entertaining reading and adds to the romance of the sport.

And of all the wildfowler's quarry, what can compare with the wild goose? These great birds wing their way to us from their breeding grounds in the distant and mysterious Arctic, riding the north wind across the oceans. Old fowlers thought that barnacle geese hatched from barnacles, hence the name. This seems incredible to us now, but we should remember that the breeding grounds of the British wintering population of our most common goose, the pinkfoot, remained unknown until as late as 1929, when they were discovered in Iceland by an expedition searching (mistakenly) for whitefronts. It was not until 1951 that the main nesting site at Thjorsarver was discovered by Peter Scott. There remains an aura of mystery about wild geese to this day.

The sheer size of the bird is impressive. A big greylag can have a wingspan of nearly 6 feet. Bagging a goose must have been a cause for celebration in the days of subsistence hunting. Even today, a fowler returning along the foreshore with a goose will find himself being stopped and congratulated by others eager to know the full story. Compare this with the counting of the bag after a day's driven pheasant shooting, with the keeper worrying about whether the Guns will have accounted for only 270 birds instead of the 300 they have paid for. This is not to denigrate driven shooting, which calls for a high degree of organisation and marksmanship; it simply illustrates how the emphasis falls on different aspects.

Even the call of the wild goose places it in a special category. It varies by species, but that of the pinkfoot is especially musical. Many have attempted to describe the emotions that it can stir. Typically, BB does it best:

> I do not think that any man who has a spark of imagination within him can fail to be moved by the almost unearthly music of a large skein of wild geese upon the wing.
>
> In remote country districts of England, especially those inland and far away from any river or estuary where these noble birds congregate, the clamour of geese passing over, often at dead of night during the migrating seasons, causes much disquiet and concern in the rustic mind and is the source of many legends. The inland villagers still regard these heavenly voices as the clamour of ghost hounds, or of evil spirits in full demoniac cry through the upper darkness. Shepherds on lonely hilltops are especially prone to these superstitious tales, and they will never believe that the sounds they hear with so much dread are but the signal cries and squadron orders of migrating birds.
>
> The reader may think that this statement is far-fetched, that I am romancing, but I can assure him that what I say is true; I have met many old villagers who believe that to hear the ghost hounds bodes ill to them and all mankind.
>
> On the coast, as might be guessed, the sound of wild geese passing in the night causes no comment. The villagers of the Wash or Humber districts would make fun of such silly old wives' tales.
>
> Yet the fact remains that there is no sound in nature so unearthly and, to my mind, more lovely, than that of the passing skeins, especially if you hear them, as they should be heard, in the quiet of a starlit winter's night, perhaps from some lonely hilltop or upland pasture. It is a most unbirdlike sound, and is rightly likened to the cry of hounds, yet no hound on earth possesses that celestial chiming voice which is so characteristic of the clamour made by a large skein of Pinkfooted geese. No bird in the vast company has an identical call, some are high-pitched, others are deep and resonant, some cry out all together, others call singly. Mostly the birds are invisible, and are perhaps a great height above the earth. You hear the melodious baying drawing nearer and ever nearer, and then gradually die away in the distance, and even I, a hardened Longshore gunner, cannot listen to that magic music unmoved.

Given a dose of prose like that, many an impressionable youngster will be hooked on the spot, as I was.

Another attractive aspect of wildfowling – especially today – is the sport's long history of active participation in conservation. In this it shares much

BB aged about 80. 'It was BB and writers like him who gently set out the ethics and conventions of the sport.'
(Tom Quinn)

with other field sports, of course, but in few other areas is the relationship between hunters and conservationists so harmonious. Some of the greatest naturalists and conservationists of our time were brought up with a love of wildfowling – or at the very least with an appreciation of it as a worthy pursuit. Sportsmen-naturalists like Abel Chapman put their acute powers of observation to good use, as did later generations: the distinct Greenland race of whitefronted goose was first described by two wildfowlers, Peter Scott and Christopher Dalgety, while the preferred food of this subspecies was discovered by another inquisitive wildfowler, Arthur Cadman. Christopher Dalgety and many other wildfowlers were also heavily involved in setting up early wildfowl surveying techniques, and to this day wildfowlers are noted for their co-operation with annual wildfowl counts and other forms of research.

The inextricable link between wildfowl and wild places has led many wildfowlers to work for the protection of wetlands and other wildfowl environments. There is a growing realisation that wildfowl are extraordinarily adept at looking after themselves – it is their habitat which needs to be preserved. Sporting interests have played a major role in creating and maintaining many important wildfowl refuges, notably Holkham,

Rockcliffe and Loch Leven. More recently, some of our most important and successful coastal nature reserves have come about through the joint efforts of responsible wildfowlers and conservationists, including those at Caerlaverock, the Humber, Southport and Lindisfarne. Many other reserves and refuges have been initiated by wildfowlers and it was Dr Jeffrey Harrison, a noted wildfowler, who pioneered schemes for utilising disused gravel pits as wildfowl habitat.

Peter Scott eventually gave up shooting, but it is interesting to note his prime reason for selecting the Slimbridge area as the founding site for the forerunner of the WWT. In his autobiography, *The Eye of the Wind*, he writes:

> The first, and perhaps the most important advantage of this area over almost all other goose resorts in Britain was the Manorial Right of the Berkeley family over the foreshore to the centre of the river channel at low water.
>
> On this right the continued existence of this large flock of whitefronts mainly depended (and still depends). The geese were preserved for shooting, but the numbers of geese shot and the amount of disturbance caused by the shooting were very small. The Berkeley Goose Shoot had been conducted in a reasonable and moderate manner ever since guns were invented; the geese owed their long and continued sanctuary to this sporting interest.

Nor should it be forgotten that the single most effective measure in restricting the shooting of excessive bags – the statutory ban on the sale of dead wild geese, which came into effect in January 1968 – was promoted by the wildfowling fraternity in the form of the Wildfowlers' Association of Great Britain and Northern Ireland (WAGBI). Founded in 1908 by Stanley Duncan, WAGBI evolved into the British Association for Shooting and Conservation (BASC), which in 1996 had more than 112,000 members. At that time there were more than 200 wildfowling clubs affiliated to the BASC, with a combined membership in excess of 15,000 – and many clubs had waiting lists.

At local level, dedicated members of wildfowling clubs across the land spend their precious free time patrolling reserves, digging ponds, planting suitable vegetation, participating in wildfowl surveys and raising money for the purchase or leasing of prime habitat. Hundreds of thousands of duck (chiefly mallard) are reared and released.

During the 1960s and early 1970s, wildfowling clubs took the lead in reintroducing greylag geese to many areas of the country. The Lake District and Norfolk are just two areas where these efforts had considerable success. Earlier, around 1930, the Earl of Stair established a breeding nucleus of greylags at his estate near Stranraer, in south-west Scotland, which supplied stock for other reintroductions and natural recolonisation throughout the area.

Today, the estate is home to a considerable breeding colony and satellite colonies have been spawned up to 40 miles away – all brought about by a combination of conservation and sporting interests which, in this instance as in so many others, proved to be of one mind.

In 1986 the BASC established an independent conservation fund, the Wildlife Habitat Trust, which funds conservation projects and land purchases in Britain. In this way, it has helped several wildfowling clubs to buy important areas of marsh and foreshore. This trust has also been used to assist projects concerning the overseas breeding and staging areas of our wildfowl.

In the Preface to the BASC's tome, *The New Wildfowler* (third edition, 1989), Sir Peter Scott pointed out that wildfowlers, naturalists, artists and others all have a common interest, and should work together. He concluded: 'So long as these bonds of common interest remain, the future of wildfowl and wildfowling is, I believe, assured; and with the same excitement of anticipation on a wild morning long hence our grandchildren will be able to see the skeins of wild geese coming in from the shore'.

Ian Pitman understood the excitement generated by wild geese, as do all wildfowlers. The final paragraph of *And Clouds Flying* begins:

> I stood, in Germany, behind the barbed wire fence that was my prison and watched a skein travelling north, arrow sharp against a green gold sunset sky. Reality faded, and I had a glimpse of the open sea, with the breakers combing in, listened to the wind howling past, felt the sting of driving sand and the tang of the salt spray, and I knew then, in its essence, the meaning of freedom.

Geese can affect people like that. During the long, dull days of high summer my goose fever is in remission and I turn to fishing. My thoughts are of butter-yellow trout sipping flies from the surface of crystal chalk streams. On these warm, humid, almost tropical afternoons, with the droning of bees faintly audible above the sound of gently sliding water, geese are the last thing on my mind. The geese themselves are far away, on their breeding grounds in the frost-shattered wastes of Iceland and eastern Greenland – a world away from the lush water-meadows of southern England.

But one day, perhaps in mid-September, the trout will be dour and sulky, refusing to rise to any of my offerings. A sudden breath of wind will send a catspaw of ripples racing across the pool, causing a momentary shiver among the leaves of the overhanging willows. A single leaf, spotted with yellow near the edges, will flutter onto the water.

That night the stars shine more brightly than usual. The flooding mass of clean, rain-filtered polar maritime air, driven by a gentle north-westerly falling calm by midnight, might allow a ground frost in the more sheltered chalk valleys.

Six hundred miles away, in Iceland, the first snow flurries of winter slither and twist across the ground in the icy breeze. Clouds run aground on Hofsjokull, the vast icecap which broods over the marshy oasis of Thjorsarver. There, down among the dwarf willow, the simple nests are deserted now, losing their last scraps of down to the scouring wind.

Most of the pinkfeet have congregated in a few traditional staging areas by now, while the more stately greylags are still scattered on the lowlands around the coastal fringe, where the snow has yet to fall.

The pinkfeet are restless. Visibility is good and the wind is favourable. Parties of geese fly uncertain circuits and land again with much gabbling. More geese take to the air as dusk gathers and then still more; this time, they remain airborne. Wheeling and breasting the wind to gain height, calling incessantly, the great birds sweep and swirl. Then the family parties begin to shake out into larger formations. With much clamour, they form and reform into wavering skeins, braiding across the luminous evening sky, and start to climb. Squadron after squadron crosses the foaming Icelandic coast, all heading on the same bearing – south-east – aiming to fly over hundreds of miles of heaving grey seas towards the distant land where they will spend the winter, just as their ancestors have done for thousands of years.

That night, as I strip the fly lines from the reels, I find myself ringing Martin to discuss plans for the winter. 'I've been thinking about geese,' I say, with barely a word of greeting. 'Same here,' he replies, as if waking from a deep sleep.

The geese are coming.

CHAPTER TWO

The Natural History of Geese

There are three very good reasons for knowing about the natural history of the quarry. First, no one will ever be a really accomplished goose shooter until he understands the habits and nature of geese. Secondly, gaining an appreciation of geese in their natural environment will in itself provide the basis for an enjoyable pastime. And thirdly, on a rather more practical point, without a very clear idea of how to identify legal quarry, the novice could end up making an error which will cost him dearly and, even worse, help to bring our sport into disrepute.

To the wildfowler, geese are much more than mere feathered targets, as we have seen. Non-shooting friends are sometimes surprised when I spend happy hours simply watching birds, armed with nothing more lethal than a pair of binoculars. Interestingly, my shooting friends are much less likely to raise their eyebrows. A birdwatcher can gain a great deal of fulfilment from observing and learning about birds, but I can do that *and* go shooting, which is an additional experience. In *The Eye of the Wind,* Sir Peter Scott's retrospective view of wildfowling seems to acknowledge this factor. He wrote:

If I were advising a young boy I would say to him: 'Of course you will enjoy wildfowling; it will bring you unequalled thrills, and if you never experience those thrills you will probably never enjoy the birds themselves to quite the same extent, for you will not learn the subtle goose/rook, wigeon/starling distinction, the subtle difference between man's attitude to his traditional quarry and his attitude to all other birds.'

It is obvious that ducks and geese are closely related. Yet there are some significant differences, of which the most basic are that geese tend to be much larger than ducks, with proportionately longer necks, legs and wings, and whereas most duck are largely aquatic in habit, most geese spend the majority of their time on land. Another chief behavioural difference is that most geese roost during the hours of darkness and feed by day – the exact opposite of most ducks. Finally, most geese are grazing birds, so they tend to have less spatulate bills than ducks.

By tradition, the geese which we find in Britain are divided into two main groups for the purpose of identification: the so-called black geese, and the grey geese. Only one species of black goose is legal quarry, while three species of grey goose may be shot.

Black Geese

The black geese comprise Canada, barnacle and brent geese, of which only the Canada is currently legal quarry. This makes identification relatively simple, because most of us are reasonably familiar with the Canada from the semi-tame flocks that frequent parks and gardens. All one has to remember is never to raise a gun to a goose with black in it unless one is absolutely sure that it is a Canada! Naturally, poor light and driving sleet, with the birds whipping past in a gale, tend to make things a little more difficult, so it is important to be able to make the correct identification from a number of clues.

The first of these clues is the bird's voice. Most geese are very vocal, and the 'a-honk' call of the Canada is quite distinctive. The call of the barnacle is very different – a sort of yapping noise; it has been said that a flock of barnacle geese sound like a pack of agitated pekinese dogs. The brent goose, on the other hand, makes a rolling 'rrronk' noise, which is rather low in tone yet carries a surprisingly long distance.

The next clue is location. Canadas are found throughout the inland areas of England, and also in one or two coastal areas, notably in northern Norfolk and near the border at the eastern end of the Solway. They are much less widespread in Scotland, although there are isolated colonies in south-western Scotland and eastern Perthshire. Barnacles, on the other hand, are seldom found far from the coast. They frequent the merse and fine grass 'lawns' which grow on shell sand. In contrast to the Canada, the barnacle is fairly rare south of the Scottish border, except in Northumberland, where a few regularly stop over at Lindisfarne on their way across to the Solway. Brent geese are even less likely to be found far from the coast, being birds of the tideline and foreshore. Their favourite food is a seaweed called zostera (also known as eel grass), although since the mid-1970s a growing number of brent have taken to raiding winter cereal crops grown just inland of the sea wall. Brent are common in parts of south-east England, particularly the estuaries of Essex, although there are also notable concentrations in the Humber, the Solent and the Wash. Lindisfarne hosts an isolated wintering population of the pale-bellied brent, a distinct subspecies from the much commoner dark-bellied brent.

On paper, Canadas and barnacles may look rather similar, but in the flesh the two birds are very different. The very much larger Canada has a black neck and brown upper wings and belly, with white being restricted to the chinstrap and the tail coverts. It is the largest of our geese, with big ganders weighing as much as 15 lb (6.8 kg), although the normal range is about 9–12 lb (4.0–5.5 kg). These birds also seem to have proportionately longer necks than our other geese. Barnacles, on the other hand, look much more obviously piebald. In certain lighting conditions their white bellies and faces are particularly conspicuous. They are much smaller than Canadas, weighing around 4–5 lb (1.8–2.7 kg). They often look rather tubby and compact. Brent are smaller still, not much bigger than a drake mallard, and commonly weigh about 3 lb (1.4 kg). They have sooty-black heads and necks, and this coloration, together with the streamlining of the head and short beak, gives this part of their anatomy a rather reptilian appearance. In flight they show a strong contrast between their generally dark plumage and their white tail coverts. Their legs seem to be shorter and set further back than those of other geese, and they fly with more rapid wingbeats.

Grey Geese

The grey geese comprise the greylag, pinkfooted, whitefronted and bean geese. Greylags and pinkfeet are legal quarry throughout Britain, and form the vast bulk of all geese bagged, so we shall examine them in more detail. The whitefront may be shot in England and Wales but *not* in Scotland, for reasons we shall discuss later. The bean goose is now rare in Britain, and is completely protected.

The easiest voice to identify belongs to the greylag, because it sounds very similar to that of the farmyard goose. The contact call is a rather nasal, some-times even guttural, 'ahnk-ung', with the second syllable being shorter and higher-pitched than the first. By contrast, the pinkfoot call has a much higher tone, also disyllabic, giving a sound which has been described as 'qwink-wink'. The situation gets a bit confused with big flocks of grey geese, because not only do individual birds display high and low notes which overlap the norm for each species, but there may also be isolated individu-als from other species flying among them. The whitefront makes a fairly melodious noise which sounds a little like a high-pitched giggle or whinny. It often has more syllables than the basic greylag or pinkfoot call, and has what I can only describe as a squeaky quality to it. It has been called a laugh-ing sound, and may be described as 'wicka-wick', being intermediate in tone between the higher-pitched pinkfoot call and the lower-pitched greylag. The bean goose is said to call much less frequently than others, with a noise that is similar to the pinkfoot but deeper and coarser.

The greylag is our largest grey goose, and exceptional specimens have tipped the scales at 12 lb (5.5 kg), although the normal range is 7–8 lb (3.2–3.6 kg). Greylags have large, thick orange-yellow bills, of the same pro-portions as farmyard geese, and relatively chunky heads. The bill is a surpris-ingly visible feature, even when the bird is flying. Some individuals have a few white feathers around the base of the bill, and old-stagers tend to have a few black blotches or bars on their grey bellies. Their backs are light brown, while their forewings are light grey, and can look lavender blue in sunlight. This feature may be very noticeable when the bird is flying. Their legs are generally a fleshy pink colour. Greylags are common worldwide, and our birds are characteristic of the western race. There is also an eastern race, which is generally slightly larger and paler with a longer, pinker bill, but this is rare in Britain; some specimens are occasionally reported in Kent, but these may be descendants of resident reintroduced birds which originated from the eastern race.

The pinkfoot is generally a smaller, lighter bird than the greylag, com-monly weighing 5½–7 lb (2.0–3.2 kg). Pinkfeet seem rather dainty com-pared with greylags, and have notably shorter and smaller bills, coloured black and pink. They appear to have finer, less bulbous heads than greylags, an impression which is particularly marked when seen at a distance because the pinkfoot's head and neck graduate into a dark, chocolate-brown colour. Although they also have grey forewings, the contrast with the rest of their plumage is not as marked as it is in the case of the greylag. Not surprisingly, pinkfeet have pink legs – although, like all geese, the colour of the legs and bill does tend to fade or change after death.

Whitefronts have orange legs. This is an important distinguishing feature, because it is only the adults which have the distinctive white foreheads and bellies heavily barred and mottled with black or very dark brown. A first winter whitefront can look very much like a rather dark, smooth greylag or a dull pinkfoot, and it is important to know the difference – especially in Scotland, where whitefronts are protected because there they are predominantly of the internationally scarce Greenland subspecies. Whitefronts are generally smaller than greylags, with an average weight in the range 4–7 lb (1.8–3.2kg) although, like all geese, individual birds may vary considerably. European whitefronts may be distinguished by their shorter, pinkish bills, while the protected Greenland whitefronts tend to be slightly larger and darker, and have longer orange or yellow bills. You are most unlikely to come across the very rare lesser whitefront, which is similar to the European whitefront but smaller and more compact – almost duck-like – with an average weight of just 3½ lb (1.6 kg). Adults also have proportionately larger white patches on their foreheads than other whitefronts, in addition to a distinctive yellow ring around the eye.

The bean goose looks very similar to the pinkfoot, although it is generally a good deal larger, often weighing 7–8 lb (3.2–3.6 kg), sometimes more. Bean geese have notably longer bills than pinkfeet, and these tend to be black and orange or yellow, rather than black and pink (there are several subspecies with slight variations in colour). Their heads seem larger and more angular, and the bird generally lacks the pinkfoot's daintiness. At a distance, bean geese look rather brown. They have orange-coloured legs.

Distribution

All the grey geese feed on agricultural land, sometimes well inland. Wintering greylags frequent many areas of Scotland, particularly the central zone, Fife and Angus, the north east, Caithness and Orkney. Migratory greylags also frequent isolated areas of England, particularly in the north and parts of the east. In addition, there are numerous reintroduced flocks in various parts of the country. Pinkfeet are also common in east central and north-east Scotland, although in addition there are major concentrations in north-west England (particularly near the Ribble estuary) and north Norfolk. European whitefronts are found in southern and south-west England, while the Greenland subspecies is found in south-west Scotland and the Western Isles (especially Islay). A few are also found wintering in one or two parts of Wales (where, incidentally, the local wildfowling clubs generally observe a self-imposed ban on shooting them). I have often seen small family parties of Greenland whitefronts 'tagging on' to larger flocks of greylags near Dunragit in south-west Scotland, and I have also seen a single Greenland whitefront flying with a flock of greylags in eastern Perthshire. Bean geese are reduced to only a couple of regular overwintering flocks – one in Norfolk's Yare valley, and another in the Carron Valley in central

Scotland – although isolated individuals may occur in flocks of other grey geese.

Identification

It can be difficult to distinguish the various species of grey goose under field conditions. Good colour photographs help, but by far the best way to learn to identify each species is to visit a reserve or a wildfowl collection with a pair of binoculars. By simply looking and listening you will learn more about practical recognition in three hours at a reserve than you can from any book, and you can also practise your ability to judge range – although you should use common sense, or you might get some odd looks from other visitors! I have spent many happy hours at the various WWT reserves and centres around the country, and I strongly recommend you to join this excellent organisation. In addition, the chart (on page 28) may help you to memorise the principal points of differentiation; you can photocopy it and keep a waterproofed version with you in the field.

If you find a particularly odd looking specimen, it is worth remembering that hybrids do sometimes occur, one of the most common being a Canada/greylag cross.

Once you have a good idea of what the various species look and sound like, and some knowledge of the sort of habitat and localities you are likely to find them in, you have little excuse for raising your gun to a protected species. None the less, if you are a novice, you should really be accompanied by an experienced fowler.

There are three other types of bird which you could mistake for a quarry goose: the swan, the cormorant and the shelduck. You may find it strange that anyone could mistake a flying swan for a goose, but it has happened – although the only case that I personally know of involved overseas visitors, who were duly reported by the head of the local wildfowling club. The cormorant is rather more understandable, especially in poor visibility. They are about the size of a goose, with similar wingbeats, although they are also generally silent and have a more balanced outline than the long-neck/short tail silhouette of the goose. Cormorants can turn up in the most unexpected places, sometimes flying along very small streams well inland. Hawker used to refer to 'lowering a parson', a peculiarly appropriate term which was the slang of his age for shooting a cormorant. They are far from being an endangered species, and many fishermen think they do too much damage to inland fisheries, but the law is the law so you must not shoot them. The shelduck is only really likely to be found on the coast, where it may be locally common. These protected duck are nearly the size of a goose and, coming head-on towards you in poor light, they can look very goose-like, although they have shallower wingbeats.

	SPECIES	RANGE	HABITAT	CALL	SIZE	BILL	LEGS	COLOUR
GREY GEESE	GREYLAG Quarry	Scotland - especially east central zone, north east, Caithness. Also resident birds in north west and south west Scotland and many parts of England, including Norfolk and Lake District.	Coast, farmland, inland waters. Family groups and small flocks, occasionally large flocks.	Guttural "ahnk-ung"	Large, chunky, with a prominent head and thick neck.	Orange/yellow, heavy and prominent	Normally flesh-coloured, but occasionally pale yellow	Grey/brown, with very light grey upper forewings. Often some dark flecks on belly and some white feathers around base of bill.
	PINKFOOT Quarry	As Greylag in Scotland, Norfolk, Humber and SW Lancashire.	Coast, farmland, inland waters. Large flocks.	Higher pitched "qwink-wink"	Medium, more rounded and lighter build than Greylag.	Small, delicate black and pink	Pink	Grey/brown, with brown neck.
	WHITEFRONT Quarry in England and Wales only - PROTECTED IN SCOTLAND	European race frequents coast of southern and south west England. Greenland race found in western and south west Scotland.	Coast, farmland, bogs, inland waters. Small or medium flocks. Occasionally with other species.	Musical, squeaky, high pitched "wicka-wick" or "wicka-wicka-wick" on ascending scale.	Medium	Medium length, pink (European) or orange/yellow (Greenland).	Orange	Grey/brown. Adults have prominent white foreheads and dark barred and blotched bellies.
	BEAN Protected	Yare valley in Norfolk, Carron valley in central Scotland, Threave in Galloway.	Coast, farmland, inland waters. Small flocks. Occasionally with other species.	Coarser version of Pinkfoot call	Medium, sometimes large.	Longer than Pinkfoot's, black and orange or yellow (varies)	Orange	Rather more brown than other grey geese.
BLACK GEESE	CANADA Quarry	Widespread throughout southern, central and northern England. Some in Scotland.	Parkland, farmland, inland waters. Family groups and small or medium sized flocks.	"A-honk"	Very large	Black	Black	Brown with paler breast and black neck with prominent white chinstrap
	BARNACLE Protected	Western Isles. western Scotland, eastern Solway. Passes through Lindisfarne	Coast, merse. Large, dense flocks.	High pitched yapping, like small dogs	Medium, compact	Black	Black	Black and white, with white face.
	BRENT Protected	Coasts of southern and eastern England.	Coast, mudflats, occasionally cereal crops just inland.	Deep, rolling, gutteral "rronk"	Small, duck-like	Black	Black	Black and dark grey with white stern.

Finally, you should be aware that several exotic species of goose have established themselves in parts of the country in recent years, mostly as a result of straying from wildfowl collections. In 1992 Simon Delaney reported the findings of a survey undertaken the previous summer, revealing a total of more than 900 Egyptian geese (a type of sheldgoose) in Britain, mostly concentrated in Norfolk. Other species recorded included barnacles (over 800), snow geese (140) and even 83 bar-headed geese!

One of the golden rules of shooting is that *you must never fire at a target unless you can positively identify it as a legitimate quarry species* – and I really do mean *positively identify*. This means that the onus is on the shooter to make absolutely sure, with no uncertainty whatsoever, that it really is a legal quarry. If ever you find yourself having to make a snap decision when you have even the slightest doubt, then whatever you do, *do not shoot!*

I was once very glad of this rule. I was on the foreshore at Lindisfarne in October, waiting for greylags to flight back to the mudflats in the evening. I had arrived in the late afternoon, and walked some way along the foot of the sea wall in the company of two ardent birdwatchers, who were festooned with expensive cameras and optical equipment. They went on up the beach towards the beacons, while I settled into a driftwood hide just below the crest of the sea wall. The sun was fairly warm and I was well wrapped up, so I fell into a light sleep. It was nearly dark when I awoke.

I was staring out into the western glow, looking across fields of winter barley, when I suddenly became aware of half a dozen geese heading straight for me, not 20 yards off the ground. Instantly, I was wide awake, flooded with adrenalin. I cocked the hammers of the eight-bore and willed the geese to keep on their course. They did. They were 60 yards away and closing as I began to lift the gun. I do not think I have ever had such an easy chance on the foreshore. The geese were silent as they came on, and I strained my eyes to make a positive identification. They were certainly not brent – so were they greylags? I decided that they must be. I was just about to heave the barrels up when I hesitated; something about them was not quite right. They somehow lacked the bulk of greylags, and why were they not calling? On the other hand, small groups of geese often fly without calling. I held my fire. They swished right over me and instantly disappeared into the dark portion of the sky behind me, heading for the tideline. I could have kicked myself.

At that exact moment, there was a rustling beside me. It proved to be the two birdwatchers, who had been walking back in the dark. They had slowed down on reaching the area where they knew I was hiding, and had also seen the geese. Very decently, they had crouched down so as not to spoil my shot (or get in the way?). 'Too far for those greylags?' enquired one.

'Er, yes,' I said rather lamely. Frankly, I would not really have wanted to shoot a goose in front of a birdwatcher, but at the same time they had unwittingly confirmed that I had indeed missed an ideal opportunity at a legal quarry. We chatted for a while, and then they moved on. I also packed up, as it was now too dark to shoot.

As I stumbled along the wall I had another surprise; there was another fowler just 75 yards along from my position. It turned out that he had arrived there while I was asleep, and had not seen me. 'Did you see those bloody geese?' I said. 'Had 'em right over me, but for some reason I just didn't fire'. The other fowler snorted. 'Just as well you didn't,' he said. 'They were barnacles!' He had been watching them through binoculars as they fed two fields away before the sun went down. I should point out that I had not seen a barnacle at Lindisfarne for two seasons. These ones had probably stayed for just one night on their way across to Caerlaverock.

I dread to think what would have happened if I had dropped a protected bird right at the feet of the birdwatchers! It was no real consolation to realise that they had also made an initial error of identification. I just thanked my lucky stars that I had obeyed my instincts and held fire – and all because there was a tiny element of doubt. The real lesson of this story is simple: if in doubt, do not shoot! The problem was not necessarily the amount of light – I have often shot under the moon when it was relatively easy to identify the quarry – it was more to do with the quality of the light, which combined with other circumstances to make positive identification almost impossible. If you ever find yourself in a similar situation, then you really have only two options; either pack up or resign yourself to simply enjoying the fresh air!

Resident Goose Populations

Most of our main quarry geese are migrants, visiting Britain for the winter. The exceptions are our resident Canadas and native greylags.

Originally introduced to Charles II's ornamental wildfowl collection more than 300 years ago, our Canadas are derived from one or more of the larger subspecies of Canada geese native to North America. By the mid-1800s feral flocks had spread throughout England, being found chiefly on parkland in private estates. They had reached Scotland by the Second World War, but it was not until the post-war years that the Canada population really took off. These sedentary birds were deliberately dispersed in small groups across the country, being introduced to many areas either as a novelty or a sporting proposition. Many wildfowling clubs were only too happy to take surplus birds and establish them in suitable habitat, assisted by the then Wildfowl Trust. This assisted dispersal allowed the Canada to exploit new territories in a way that the species had not managed on its own. The gravel pits and reservoirs associated with the economic growth of the post-war years, especially the late 1960s, provided ideal roosting and nesting sites. From an estimated population of 2,600–3,600 birds in 1953, our Canada numbers surged to about 10,000 in the late 1960s. By then, the population seemed to have reached some form of critical mass, and began to rise exponentially. By 1981 it was estimated at nearly 20,000, by 1985 it was 39,000, in the early 1990s it exceeded 60,000, and now some authorities predict that it could reach as much as 100,000 shortly after the year 2000. Canada geese are now serious pests in many areas, especially parkland and campsites, where they foul the ground. They may also be starting to compete with resident greylag populations.

Our resident breeding greylags are the remnants of a much larger native population which was gradually depleted as the marshes and meres were drained and the remaining birds were hunted for food. The greylag used to breed all over Britain, but by the early 1800s it had become uncommon everywhere – even in its East Anglian stronghold – and by the early 1900s the breeding population was restricted to north-west Scotland and the Western Isles. Even here the greylag was persecuted mercilessly, not least by crofters, who accused it of wrecking oat fields. By the early 1950s there were probably only a couple of hundred breeding pairs left with a total population of perhaps 1,000, but better statutory protection and changing attitudes led to a great improvement in the greylag's fortunes, and populations have since grown steadily. In addition, wildfowling clubs and interested landowners have helped to reintroduce the species to many of its former haunts, as we saw in Chapter 1. In 1991 the reintroduced greylag population was censused at 19,000 (with an estimated total of 22,000) and seemed to be in a healthy state, although there is some evidence that its previously steady rate of increase is now slowing.

Some people refer to all reintroduced greylags as 'feral', but this can be misleading; the reintroduced birds are usually of the same genetic stock as our native breeders, and remain wild and wary. For example, the flock reintroduced by the Earl of Stair originated from native Hebridean stock. On the other hand, a small number of our greylags really are feral, being semi-tame birds that have escaped from collections.

Migratory Goose Populations

Geese are no respecters of international boundaries, and many species breed across broad swaths of the Arctic and subarctic, wintering in a variety of countries right around the northern hemisphere. Whitefronts, for instance, are found in North America (where they are often called 'speckle-bellies'), while brent winter on both sides of the North American continent, being known over there as 'brant'. For the sake of simplicity, we shall concentrate on the geese which regularly visit Britain.

In winter, our native greylags are joined by their migratory cousins from Iceland. We also get the Icelandic population of pinkfeet, which is itself bolstered by a smaller population of pinkfeet from eastern Greenland. Pinkfeet also breed in Spitsbergen, but this population – which is only about one fifth the size of the Icelandic one – is entirely separate and winters in Denmark, the Netherlands and Belgium. During very hard winters, it is possible that small numbers of these birds may reach southern England.

We also host a considerable proportion of the world's barnacle geese, a species which breeds in four separate areas of the Arctic. The Siberian and Swedish breeding populations winter in the Netherlands and Germany, while the entire Spitsbergen population winters at Caerlaverock, on the Solway. The barnacles which breed in north-east Greenland winter in Ireland and Scotland – chiefly on Islay and several other islands off the west coast.

Another migratory goose of which we host an internationally important wintering population is the Greenland whitefront, which breeds in western Greenland. The entire population of this subspecies winters in the British Isles – about half in Ireland and the rest Scotland, with a few in Wales. The internationally much more numerous European whitefront, which nests right across Arctic Eurasia, winters in several areas of Scandinavia and north-west Europe, with only a relatively small number reaching England. Hence, this goose is not protected, even though it is not particularly populous in Britain during the winter, while the Greenland whitefront, which is locally abundant in Scotland, is protected because the world population of this subspecies is relatively small and possibly endangered.

The brent goose breeds right up in the high Arctic. The pale-bellied subspecies of brent that visits Lindisfarne in the winter belongs to the Spitsbergen and Franz Josef Land breeding population. This population usually spends the early part of the winter in Denmark before moving to Lindisfarne for the second half of the season. At times, the count at Lindisfarne reaches 3,000. We host much higher numbers of dark-bellied brent, which breed along the coast of Arctic Siberia and winter in several countries of north-west Europe in addition to Britain.

Our few wintering bean geese are thought to come from a population which breeds in northern Sweden and regularly visits Jutland (often not appearing in Britain until December). Bean geese are internationally abundant, with several distinct subspecies breeding right across northern Eurasia. The bean goose used to be the most common of all the geese wintering in Britain, but a decline set in during the mid-1800s, possibly due to changes in agricultural practice. Over recent decades the number of bean geese wintering in Britain has generally been just a few hundred. The pinkfoot (which may be a western subspecies of the bean) seems to have filled the ecological niche left by the bean goose, although there is little doubt that early observers often failed to distinguish between the two species, so it is difficult to be sure of exactly what happened.

So, with the exception of the resident greylags and Canadas, all our geese are migrants from the Arctic or subarctic. In summary, we host virtually the entire Iceland/Greenland population of pinkfeet, the vast majority of Icelandic greylags, the entire Spitsbergen and most of the Greenland populations of barnacle geese, half of the entire population of Greenland whitefronts, most of the European wintering population of light-bellied brent, about half the European wintering population of dark-bellied brent, a small proportion of European whitefronts, and a few bean geese. What an awesome responsibility! It behoves us to look after these species, which come to us for just a few months every year after breeding in faraway lands and flying vast distances across many national boundaries.

Fortunately, most goose populations are currently very healthy. As we have already seen, our resident greylags have reversed years of decline, while our Canadas have reached pest proportions and are having to be culled by a variety of means, including egg-pricking. But the really interesting populations are the migratory ones, which include the main quarry species.

Taking non-quarry geese first, the most remarkable increase is shown by the dark-bellied brent. This goose, the traditional quarry of the punt gunner in Colonel Hawker's day, plummeted to a frighteningly low European wintering population of just 16,500 in 1954 (with rather fewer in Britain) largely as a result of a natural catastrophe: its preferred food, zostera, was almost wiped out by a disease in the 1920s and 1930s. Once the population had fallen so far, any pressure from shooting or disease may have become unsustainable, given that the population has little in reserve to cope with poor breeding years. Even today, the breeding success of this high Arctic breeder is erratic, with almost total failure in years with late springs. Nonetheless, protection since 1954 and a gradual return of zostera, together with the bird's adaptation to feeding on alternative foods, has seen our wintering brent numbers soar to well over 100,000 in recent years. Indeed, some farmers in south-east England and the Netherlands now consider the bird to be a considerable agricultural pest, and compensation has had to be paid. Many wildfowlers would like the brent to be returned to the quarry list, but conservationists are still worried about its vulnerability to exceptional weather conditions. In some years, the proportion of young birds in our wintering flocks can approach as much as 50 per cent, but in others it is virtually non-existent.

The barnacle goose is another conservation success story. The Spitsbergen population, which winters exclusively on the Solway, had dwindled to around 400 in the late 1940s, partly due to overshooting. The Solway wintering population gained protection in 1954, while all barnacle geese gained complete protection in Britain in 1981. Today, the Spitsbergen barnacle population has reached new heights, with a total of 13,700 being recorded in 1994. The only problem now is that the geese are beginning to overflow the reserve at Caelaverock, giving rise to calls for the birds to be shot under licence as an agricultural pest. The concentration of wintering Greenland barnacles on Islay, which numbered some 26,000 in 1995, is also causing concern to farmers.

The increasing concentration of Greenland whitefronts on Islay is another cause for concern. The British wintering population was only about 8,000 in the 1970s, but as a result of protection in Scotland since 1981 and in Greenland a decade later, the number of these birds wintering in Britain reached 19,000 in 1994, with the vast majority of these being found on Islay. In combination with the barnacles, this high concentration of geese has placed considerable pressure on the island's agricultural resources. A few paying sportsmen have been encouraged to take advantage of crop protection licences to shoot protected geese on Islay, but I find it difficult not to agree with conservationists who insist that this represents a blatant breach of the spirit of the legislation. You may say that sport and pest control are not necessarily mutually exclusive, but this cannot apply in the case of an endangered population. The commercial element is all too likely to distort the number of applications for licences.

Of more interest to the goose shooter is the massive rise in the populations of our migratory quarry geese, with the pinkfoot leading the way. The long-term increase in the Iceland/Greenland pinkfoot population is truly remarkable. In the early 1950s, this population was estimated at around 30,000 (although this may not have been a very accurate count by modern standards). In 1994, the census revealed no less than 266,000! It seems that the availability of breeding sites in Iceland may now be reaching something like saturation point, but there may still be room for expansion in eastern Greenland – although some researchers fear this may be at the expense of the Greenland barnacle. Until recently, the chief limiting factor seems to have been the availability of food on the wintering grounds in Britain, but the growing tendency to plant winter-sown cereal crops, and the improvement of grass pasture in both Britain and Iceland may have benefited both greylags and pinkfeet. This, together with the creation of numerous reserves and refuges, seems to have effected a drop in relative mortality, allowing the population to explode.

The story is much the same with our Icelandic greylags, although here the population growth has been less spectacular, and there are definite signs that it may have peaked. The estimate of the Icelandic greylag population in the early 1950s was around 30,000 – much the same as the pinkfoot – and reached 100,000 in 1992, with a slight drop to 88,000 in 1994. Once again, changes in agricultural practice and the protection afforded by refuges seem to have favoured the greylag, although it is also worth noting that the prohibition of the sale of dead wild geese is also cited as an additional major factor in the rise of both pinkfoot and greylag populations since the late 1960s.

The fact that pinkfeet have overtaken greylags may be partly due to the relatively higher shooting mortality suffered by the latter, due to a number of behavioural factors which we shall look at later. In particular, it seems that greylags suffer greater shooting mortality in the early autumn in Iceland, where local guides now take paying Guns from other countries. In1994 the Icelandic government introduced a system for assessing the annual bags made by resident shotgunners. The results for the first season – 1995 – were astonishing; about 10,000 pinkfeet were bagged, but the greylag figure was an incredible 30,000! Presumably the Icelandic shooters are much more likely to encounter greylags rather than pinkfeet because the former are more likely to frequent lowland pastures in the early autumn.

Despite the overwhelming success of our two main quarry species, the picture is less than rosy for our wintering European whitefronts. Although the Siberian breeding population is increasing, we seem to be hosting fewer and fewer of these geese, with a wintering population of just over 5,300 in 1994, compared with perhaps 6,000–8,000 in the early 1950s. We seem to be at the edge of their natural wintering range, and there is some evidence that they are in the process of retreating eastward.

Total Numbers of Quarry Geese

Taken overall, the good news is that the total number of quarry geese resident or wintering in Britain has increased greatly over recent decades, even if some species have been removed from the quarry list. Appendix D shows an increase in the total number of quarry geese in the mid-1990s compared with the early 1950s of nearly 400 per cent.

Although the number of people shooting geese has increased since the Second World War, it is obvious that our main quarry geese populations are easily capable of absorbing the losses due to shooting. In 1996, the BASC estimated the annual winter mortality of our two main quarry species at approximately 12–13 per cent, so a very rough guess might put the annual British bag at around 10 per cent of our total wintering pinkfoot and greylag populations, or about 35,000 geese. Perhaps 700,000 people shoot live quarry in Britain, with the overwhelming majority using shotguns. Of these, the BASC estimates that perhaps 130,000 shoot wildfowl at least once a year, with perhaps 5,000–6,000 BASC members being dedicated goose shooters. Although it seems likely that the majority of goose-shooting enthusiasts will tend to be members of the BASC, the total number of goose shooters is bound to be appreciably greater. In addition, there are many goose shooters who visit us from overseas.

By international standards, the shooting pressure on our quarry geese is very light *in Britain*, and although the number of goose shooters seems set to continue rising, this is being more than balanced by the firming up of the limited individual bag philosophy, which we shall discuss in more detail in Chapter 3. The shooting mortality of geese is generally considered to be non-compensatory, that is to say, shooting geese in the winter removes a certain number of potential breeders. By contrast, many quarry duck populations suffer considerable natural winter mortality anyway, so shooting an appreciable number has no real effect on the total number surviving to breed. However, although our quarry goose populations seem more than capable of absorbing the current level of loss from shooting, the apparently enormous bag of greylags in Iceland may be a cause for concern. Certainly, our wintering population of greylags has not increased over the last decade or more, and may actually be in a gentle decline. It is difficult to see how the population can grow if the Icelandic bag really is as high as is indicated.

The Move Inland

As well as a notable increase in most goose populations and the increasing popularity of goose shooting, the sport has becoming an overwhelmingly inland pursuit, much to the dismay of the foreshore purists. There are two forces involved here. First, the change in the quarry list has limited the choice of quarry to species which happen to frequent inland habitats. In contrast, the barnacles and brent which accounted for a significant part of earlier goose shooters' bags are overwhelmingly coastal birds. Secondly, the habits of our current main quarry species – pinkfeet and greylags – have changed. Today, the vast majority of greylags roost on inland waters rather than on the mudflats, and even the more foreshore-oriented pinkfoot seems to be favouring roosts on major inland waters. *Wildfowl in Great Britain* (second edition, 1986) records that of 25 major pinkfoot roosts in east-central Scotland, only six were coastal and even there the geese moved inland to feed. Where they do still roost on the mudflats and sandbanks, pinkfeet tend to do so within reserves and refuges. In addition, both pinkfeet and greylags now tend to feed almost exclusively inland on cultivated agricultural land, whereas in previous years they used to spend at least part of their time on the saltings and the fresh marshes just behind the sea wall. Whitefronts remain the most likely to be found feeding on rough pasture and bogs, but they now form only a relatively small part of the total bag.

In *Wild Geese of the World*, Myrfyn Owen describes how the individual goose species were originally adapted to differing habitats:

Four thousand years ago more than 95 per cent of Britain was forested, so goose habitat existed only in small pockets. The greylag goose was resident in the southern fens and tidal marshes where it fed on roots and tubers of marsh plants. The pinkfooted goose was probably an estuarine species as it is largely today, grazing on the shifting sandbanks of the west coast estuaries on saltmarsh grass, and in the autumn stripping seeds from sedges and rushes on the more stable grassland. The Greenland whitefronted goose lived on the acid bogs of western Scotland, Ireland and Wales, as it does to some extent today, probing for bulbils and roots of sedges and cotton grass. It was argued that the European whitefronted goose, which also occurs at present, would have competed with the pinkfoot for sandy estuaries and was only able to colonise the country following the northward retreat of that species to use the newly available open land.

The barnacle goose grazed on very short swards, which were found on the exposed western islands of Scotland and Ireland. They also probed for clover stolons and stripped seeds from the standing stalks of sedges in autumn. The brent goose until recently remained to a large extent on its traditional habitat – the muddy estuaries of the east coast of England and Scotland, and around the Irish coast.

The Arctic Dimension

With the exception of our resident greylags and Canadas, our migratory geese are essentially Arctic birds (and of course the Canada is migratory in its native continent). They breed in the Arctic or subarctic regions, and spend as much time there (or on migration) as they do with us. Exactly why they do this is open to debate. Some theories suggest that geese were originally purely Arctic birds, and only the onset of recent ice ages pushed them south. It is known that ice-free areas remained in several locations north of the icesheets, and isolated populations could have survived there, although they would have been forced to migrate south in the winter. Others may have followed the tundra line as it fluctuated north and south.

The attraction of the far north as a place for breeding is due to a number of factors, including the virtually continuous daylight in summer. This allows unlimited feeding opportunities for breeding geese, which need to take advantage of the brief but vigorous growth of vegetation. It also allows them to keep watch for predators. The sheer expanse of the tundra, and the relatively low density of these predators – chiefly Arctic foxes, gulls and skuas – is another benefit. Another favourable factor is the physical nature of the tundra in summer. Despite the low levels of precipitation, the melting of accumulated snow and ice on ground which thaws for just a few inches on top of an impermeable layer of permafrost gives rise to a landscape of pools, bogs and marshes – a veritable goose's paradise, with myriad nesting sites.

There are drawbacks, of course, although geese have evolved in harmony with their environment and are well suited to dealing with the problems, of which the cold is perhaps the most pervasive. The high Arctic is defined as a zone where the mean temperature in the warmest month (normally July) is less than 5°C. The low Arctic boundary is marked by the 10° isotherm. Just to put this into context, high Arctic breeders could conceivably experience colder weather in the summer, when they are nesting, than when wintering in Britain! This may explain why geese are relatively unaffected by frost in this country. Only ice glazing or deep snow covering their feeding grounds for a prolonged period makes them move on.

Late springs on their nesting grounds, however, are a real problem, because there is very limited time for slippage in the hectic breeding schedule. No month is entirely frost free in the high Arctic, and even in the low Arctic the frosts tend to end in mid-June and start again at the end of August. One of the worst Arctic weather phenomena is late spring rain which freezes on contact with the surface, forming an impenetrable glaze. One of these fortunately rare events was responsible for the decimation of a snow goose population several decades ago, while another is thought to have wiped out the musk ox in some parts of the Canadian Arctic.

In 1949 Peter Scott visited the Perry River region, in Canada's North West Territories, to study breeding Ross's geese. He subsequently wrote up the diary of the expedition in the form of a book called *Wild Geese and Eskimos*. It was a late spring, and his photographs of the area in mid-June show it still almost entirely covered in snow, with unbroken sea ice offshore. He recorded showers of snow falling as late as 23 July!

Nesting geese have more leeway in subarctic regions, such as Iceland, than in truly Arctic regions further north, but even so the race to breed and fledge is a close-run thing. In a paper about pinkfeet in central Iceland written by D E Hardy and published in *Wildfowl* (the journal of the WWT, then called the Wildfowl Trust) the accepted dates for the Thjorsarver colony are given as follows:

Eggs first laid	12 May
Peak clutch completion	25 May
Peak hatching date	22 June
Non-breeders regain flight	28 July
Breeding adults regain flight	4 August
Goslings achieve flight	6–10 August

Snow normally begins to fall in the uplands of central Iceland in early September, and pinkfeet generally start their main migration to Britain in mid-September. It is astonishing to think that a bird hatched on 22 June will be capable of flying just seven or eight weeks later, and capable of completing a 600 to 800 mile non-stop journey just five or six weeks after that. Yet the migration of other geese is even more impressive.

Icelandic pinkfeet tend to nest in the interior of the country in one of two quite different types of site: on rocky promontories and ridges or cliff faces above gorges, or on hummocks raised above the water level in marshy areas. The great marshy oasis of Thjorsarver, surrounded by lava desert, hosts a breeding colony which forms perhaps 70 per cent of the Icelandic total. Some of the individual nest sites here are believed to have been in continuous use for as much as 40 years, with a considerable cup being built up by the droppings and debris of succeeding generations. The smaller population of Greenland-nesting pinkfeet tend to favour rocky sites, like the minority of their Icelandic cousins.

Icelandic greylags, by contrast, nest in smaller, more scattered colonies nearer the coastal fringe. The snow comes later to these areas, so the peak greylag migration to Britain tends to take place later than that of the pinkfoot. Our resident British greylags nest in much higher-density colonies, favouring secluded marshy areas, and in particular small wooded islands and reed beds.

In a good breeding year both pinkfeet and migratory greylags might make it to our shores with a young-bird count of up to 30 per cent, but in poor years this can fall to less than 10 per cent. There is also some evidence that as total populations rise, so clutch sizes and the proportion of birds breeding tends to decrease by some natural mechanism.

Geese are monogamous and pair for life, which seems efficient for a migratory bird with limited time to start breeding each spring. The birds are generally capable of breeding in their third year, and if a mate is lost, they usually pair up again. Both parents look after the young, of which two or three might survive to make their first migration. The young birds generally stay with the family group until the spring.

Migration

Geese probably migrate both overnight and during the day. In the case of the non-stop journey from Iceland, migrating greylags and pinkfeet fly in family groups, often teamed up in much bigger skeins, with the parents showing the young birds the way (it is interesting to note that this really is the case – geese seem to learn the route, rather than following it purely by instinct). The journey probably takes 12–20 hours at an average speed of 40–50 mph, depending on wind conditions. It used to be thought that migrating geese travelled at high altitudes and indeed, in some parts of the world they have to; migrating bar-headed geese, for instance, have been seen at 29,000 feet (8,800 metres) crossing the Himalayas. But observations of North American geese seem to suggest that our Icelandic grey geese probably fly at no more than 3,000–4,000 feet (900–1,200 metres), probably coming much lower in fog, mist or heavy rain. It is probable that lost or tired birds – especially young of the year – rest on the sea, although little is known about this.

Migrating geese seem to prefer to set off during conditions of good visibility. This may be due to their navigation systems, which are widely believed to involve an internal clock which can be synchronised to the relative position of the sun and the stars. Magnetic fields may also have some influence, and at low level visual recognition of features and landscapes is undoubtedly used for fine tuning routes. There is some evidence that geese migrating from Iceland to Britain time their departure to coincide with following winds, typically in the aftermath of a depression tracking eastward across the North Sea beyond Shetland, dragging north-westerly winds in behind it. By the same token, geese departing Britain on their return to Iceland sometimes seem to take advantage of a south-easterly airflow, such as that typically produced by an anticyclone over Britain or the North Sea.

It is amazing how regular the arrival of geese can be; it is probably linked to day-length stimulus. There are many accounts of geese appearing at traditional arrival points to within a two or three days of the same date virtually every year.

Greenland pinkfeet tend to join their Icelandic neighbours in early September, and the population as a whole normally starts to migrate to Britain in mid-September, with a peak towards the end of the month. Migration to Britain is mostly completed by mid-October. Icelandic greylags, however, generally do not start migrating to Britain at that time, their migration being largely completed by the first week in November. In Iceland they frequent the lower land around the coastal fringe, where the snow comes later than in the interior highlands. Both species tend to be highly concentrated in a few locations when they first arrive, dispersing more widely a few weeks later.

Pinkfeet make the return journey to Iceland in mid- to late April, with some birds lingering until mid-May. On arrival in Iceland they tend to feed on the lowlands for a fortnight or so before moving on into the interior as the snow melts there. Greylags tend to leave Britain in early to mid-April.

In *Tales Of A Wildfowler*, Arthur Cadman gives a delightfully evocative description of 'the end of the journey'. He and a companion had just begun packing up after a morning flight on the foreshore.

> Three miles away, on the edge of the shore there is a sudden spatter of shots and away in the north a thin black line is visible in the sky.
>
> 'Listen to those damn' fools shooting at those geese; they're a thousand feet up!'
>
> 'By jove, they're coming out though – and heading this way.'
>
> As two large bulks squeeze into a pit scarcely large enough for one, the sides seem to heave and sand grains crumble and run down the sides. Once again the miles of flat sand are empty and vacant – except for the tin decoys and a few footprints in the sand.
>
> They are dropping now, still half a mile away . . . dropping on stiff wings . . . lower and lower, losing height and swinging in towards the decoys.
>
> The morning sun, shining from behind the pit, lights up every feather of their plumage. They are calling too, answering Richard's decoy call (which is no longer full of sand!). It is evident that, out of some 5,000 acres of flat sands, they have selected the few acres we have chosen for them around the decoys. Now they are wheeling in against the slight easterly breeze. Only 20 yards high, on they come, calling, dropping . . . paddles down. The leaders are settling now and in a moment they are all down. There they are, 40 pinkfeet, all on the sand 50 yards from the tin decoys, and just out of shot of the two men, whose presence is quite unsuspected. Then after a few more calls and a few paces forward, all these geese, one after the other, tuck in their heads and go to sleep. We, the two fowlers, had been privileged to see the 'End of the Journey'. For nearly two days they had been flying, over ice cap and ocean, over mountains and rivers and northern estuaries, following the everlasting call, following the immortal air route; here, at last, once again, they have come to rest with yet another long, long migration behind them.
>
> For twenty minutes we watched them and then, as there was nothing else to be done, we stood up. There was a moment of astonished silence, followed by a loud clamour, as they took off, only to settle again (so tired were they) some half a mile away . . .

The main winter/summer movements are not the only migrations made by geese. All adult geese moult during the summer, when they are flightless for about three weeks. In many cases, non-breeding birds migrate further north to somewhere quiet for the moult, returning when they are able to fly again. Many non-breeding pinkfeet fly from Iceland to eastern Greenland for the moulting period, while it is interesting to note that some of our resident Canadas have gradually developed a moult migration within Britain. Today, an appreciable number of non-breeding Canadas, chiefly from Yorkshire, make an annual migration to the Beauly Firth in Scotland during the summer, returning at the beginning of autumn. It is not clear whether this pattern has been influenced by the original artificial dispersal of flocks.

Behaviour

Of the two main quarry species, the pinkfoot is generally held to be the more difficult to shoot, being credited with greater wariness than the slightly more ponderous greylag. In reality, this may be something to do with the fact that pinkfeet tend to fly in larger skeins, sometimes numbering several hundred. Not only is it difficult to attract skeins of that size to decoys, but the sheer number of beady eyes peering down out of the sky means that the shooter is much more likely to be detected. In addition, one may sometimes unwittingly encounter less wary feral greylags, which may give a false impression of this species as a whole. By contrast, pinkfeet are always genuinely wild birds.

Greylags tend to feed in rather smaller groups than pinkfeet, and they commonly fly in small skeins, typically consisting of family groups of perhaps four or five birds and sometimes combining in several families numbering 20 or 30 birds in total. This means that greylags are relatively more effectively decoyed than pinkfeet; not only are greylags more likely to be attracted by comparatively small spreads of decoys, but the smaller skeins are less likely to spot the hidden shooters. In addition, a succession of smaller skeins coming within shotgun range is obviously much more likely to give the opportunity of a large bag than just one or two massive skeins.

Whitefronts tend to fly in smaller groups, like greylags, but they can be very wary and difficult to decoy in certain conditions. Canadas can also be wild and wary, as they are in North America, but all too often they are too tame to be counted as proper sporting quarry. Some seldom even fly, simply walking from their roost to feed.

On arrival in Britain, grey geese tend to feed on spilled grain in stubble fields, before moving on to graze on grass, clover and finally winter-sown cereals later in the season – although grass remains their main food. They are also very fond of cleaning up harvested potato fields, especially when frost has softened the tubers, and pinkfeet have been known to damage growing carrots in Lancashire, although this is unusual. Pinkfeet also take a lot of harvested beet tops in Norfolk, and I have seen greylags feeding on standing rape in County Durham during a spell of particularly severe weather, when deep snow covered their normal feeding grounds. Geese can cause considerable damage to growing cereal crops, although not so much by pecking them down as by 'paddling up' wet fields with their feet, which can give rise to barren patches of hardened mud when drier weather comes.

The amount that geese eat varies considerably throughout the season. The doyen of goose experts, Myrfyn Owen, has calculated that a whitefront eats about 700 g per day of fresh grass in winter, which equates to perhaps one third of the bird's bodyweight. Later on in the season, this level of consumption could double, as the birds prepare for the return migration and breeding. Indeed, the condition of the bird when it returns to its breeding grounds seems to play a major factor in breeding success. Grain has a higher food value than grass, but it is normally only available to the birds for a few weeks at the beginning of the season. In the depth of winter, geese have to spend around 90 per cent of daylight hours feeding.

Geese flight out to their feeding grounds from a secure roost at dawn, returning at dusk (in the Netherlands, some greylags do the reverse, but this is very much the exception to the rule). Geese will also flight under the moon, but we shall look in much more detail at this process of flighting in Chapter 7, when we examine tactics. It is worth noting here that it is generally accepted that pinkfeet will travel much further to feed than greylags. *Wildfowl in Great Britain* (second edition) recorded that pinkfeet preferred larger, more isolated waters to roost on than greylags, and this often meant that pinkfeet had to travel further to feed. In fact, a survey showed that 15 per cent of pinkfoot feeding took place more than 10 km (6¼ miles) from the roost, and 1 per cent was more than 20 km (12½ miles) distant. By contrast, 90 per cent of greylag feeding was within 5 km (3⅛ miles) of the roost, and just 2 per cent more than 10 km (6¼ miles) away.

Greylags have a tendency to roost in smaller groups on inland waters, sometimes using quite small lakes of just a few acres. They may also roost in small parties on sandbanks along rivers or on flashes in large fields. Pinkfeet are more likely to roost on estuarine sand or mudbanks than greylags, although they also seem to favour inland waters these days, generally fairly large ones. Pinkfeet tend to roost in larger gatherings than greylags.

Geese are often credited with extraordinary powers of intelligence, but in reality this is little more than a combination of natural wariness, acute senses and experience. In captivity, grey geese have lived beyond 20 years, but the average for a wild goose in a hunted population may be only around one quarter of this. Some wild geese will live to a ripe old age, of course, but there is much evidence from observation and studies on related species of wildfowl to suggest that young birds form a disproportionate amount of the shooting casualties, presumably because they are less wary. If a goose survives its first winter, its chances of living to 10 or 15 years probably increase greatly.

Most professional goose guides have stories of isolated occasions on which normally cautious geese have behaved with almost suicidal lack of caution. On one such occasion, the well-known goose guide Percy Betts and a colleague were out among the decoys picking up dead geese when a skein approached from the air. Percy and his partner crouched down and kept still, and to their astonishment some of the geese actually landed among them. The birds only took wing when the two men stood up!

I remember shooting with another well-known goose guide, Alan Murray, near Loch Leven during a week when the weather was mild and the geese had been as wary and suspicious as ever. We had great difficulty in bagging any, but on the last day of our trip, we were set up in a potato field when the greylags just poured in. The four of us shot two each (one of which was only wing-tipped, and so added to Alan's collection) and then we sat and watched. Even when we went to pick up the decoys, the geese swirled around just 30 or 40 feet above our heads, desperate to land. Alan's theory was that they were newly arrived from Iceland, but even so there should have been a few wiser old stagers among them.

Many gunners also have tales of single geese apparently flying over to reconnoitre the hide site before it is finished, with the result that no skein flies near that morning. I have observed something very similar to this myself on several occasions, but I believe these incidents have a relatively simple explanation. Lone geese often fly earlier than the main armies in the morning, and they call constantly, weaving and circling around in an apparently aimless fashion. I believe they are often searching for a lost mate. By the time the main flight has begun, the singleton may indeed be aware of the hide, and it will, if necessary, give the alarm to any skein it has eventually joined up with if they appear to head too close to it. This is not deliberate cunning so much as basic intelligence and instinct.

I can recall an incident when several of us were hiding along the banks of a burn in south-west Scotland. The cover was poor from one angle, and as a skein of greylags approached our decoys, a single goose, flying apart from the rest, saw one of us move. The skein lost height and clearly wanted to pitch among the decoys, but the singleton was having none of it; he screamed and yelled, flying over the skein and redoubling his efforts every time they made another circuit. We were full of admiration – and a touch despondent – as the skein eventually headed off.

Feeding geese are sometimes credited with posting sentries, and some old fowlers even say they have seen geese nipping others to signify that it is their turn! Once again, there is no evidence that this is deliberate. Feeding geese often squabble and nip each other, and while the proportion of alert geese does tend to be higher on the fringes of the feeding flock, this is more a matter of circumstance and, literally, pecking order than anything else.

Geese have sharp eyesight and they can spot movement a long way off, although at times in the half-light they can be fooled remarkably easily as long as one remains still. They have acute hearing, although they do not necessarily flee from the human voice – a sound they must often hear in a variety of harmless circumstances. Contrary to what many old gunners believe, there is no evidence that geese have a well-developed sense of smell.

Once they become accustomed to it, geese are sometimes capable of putting up with some extraordinary types of disturbance. I once took great care to hide myself and some fellow shooters on a bare and desolate field next to an active military airfield, when 200 greylags and about 40 Greenland whitefronts pitched onto the neighbouring field. Suddenly a fire tender appeared on the perimeter road, with lights flashing, and passed not 200 yards from the feeding geese. They did not even look up. Then the tender started firing signal cartridges into the air to scare off flocks of sea-gulls, which duly departed. One or two of the geese put their heads up, but they must have been accustomed to this early-morning runway-clearance ritual, as they were otherwise unperturbed. But there was more to come. Two military jets screamed off the runway, nacelles glowing white hot, and flew straight over the birds at no more than 100 feet. We watched open-mouthed, expecting an appalling crash. The geese rose in a ripple as the jets passed over them, like a deep pile carpet springing up behind the sweep of a hand, then simply made one low circuit, landed back in the same spot, and carried on feeding!

Geese are remarkable fliers, as one might expect. All grey geese are capable of losing height suddenly in a spectacular fashion, an action called whiffling. When geese whiffle they side-slip, rocking and tumbling down through the air like rain-soaked autumn leaves. They sometimes do this over decoys, but more commonly when they go back to roost at night, flying right out beyond any possible danger on the shore of the loch or estuary and then plummeting down.

One of the most distinctive features of flying geese is their formation. This is often described as a v-shape, but in reality it is usually less symmetrical, more often being a chevron or bow with unequal arms, or a wavering, diagonal line. The way these formations form and re-form is fascinating, but the essential component of the formation remains the same: each bird maintains a position behind and off to one side of the one in front. Nobody really seems to know why they do this, although there are many theories. It has been said that each succeeding bird benefits aerodynamically from the wash created by the bird in front. Another explanation is that the

45

birds are keeping in visual contact in the most efficient formation. Yet flying geese usually call continuously, so why do they not keep in contact like that? It is possible that the answer lies in a combination of the two theories.

Legend has it that a skein is always led by a seasoned veteran, an old gander who has seen it all before. For this reason, it is sometimes said that one should never shoot the lead goose, but to choose another bird, which will make a more tender meal. Yet if you watch a skein carefully through binoculars, you can see that the lead often changes every few minutes. It may be that older birds tend to take the lead more often, but plenty of young geese have been shot from the front of skeins.

Sexing and Ageing Geese

Telling the age and sex of a goose is not particularly easy, even in the hand. Unlike most birds, geese do not have distinct male and female plumage, nor are the sexes particularly unequal in size, especially in view of the fairly wide range of size and coloration between individuals of the same sex and species.

As a rough guide, younger geese are less boldly marked than older birds, with less clearly defined edges to the main feathers and a generally duller, more mottled appearance. Their bills and legs also tend to be less highly coloured. For the first few months of winter the tip of the young bird's tail feathers will have a little v-shaped notch in it. Young greylags lack the dark belly flecks of older birds, and seldom have white feathers at the base of their bills. Young whitefronts totally lack the adult's white forehead, and have rather dull bellies without any of the adult's prominent black bars and blotches. Finally, all young birds tend to be rather smaller and lighter than older birds.

Ganders tend to be larger than their mates, and are generally more aggressive in behaviour – especially when feeding. It is not difficult to tell the two sexes apart when they are seen together, but identifying single or dead birds is less easy. If you do have a bird in the hand, gentle pressure on either side of the cloaca should tend to evert the male's penis, although this is relatively inconspicuous in a first-winter bird.

I would urge you to keep a record of your bag, including such details as location, date, time, weather, weight, relative age, sex, condition, and some basic body measurements. I also try to note the number of cartridges I fire at each flight. All you need is a measuring tape, a set of fisherman's scales, and a notebook and pencil. Recording the details of each bagged goose on a pre-drawn chart should take just a couple of minutes. Apart from the fascination of looking up old records, and perhaps recalling particular flights, you never know when your records will contribute to some form of research.

CHAPTER THREE

Etiquette

In goose shooting, etiquette means the accepted customs of correct behaviour. Wildfowlers are not overly fond of formality and protocol, being generally a rather independent-minded bunch. Yet goose shooting gives rise to strong emotions and personal opinions, and normally taciturn wildfowlers are not at all shy in denouncing practices which they think are harmful to their sport. In this their motives are admirable, but fear of upsetting the old hands may sometimes deter novices who are genuinely interested in goose shooting but do not know the form.

The etiquette of goose shooting is not set in stone, nor is it even described fully in a printed code. Like the British constitution, it is unwritten, and subject to interpretation and change as circumstances alter. For this reason we should not become too dogmatic about precisely what is or is not acceptable, so long as the underlying principles are maintained. I would define these principles as being linked to respect: for our quarry, our fellow sportsmen, the environment and other people who care about geese. From this fundamental consideration spring all sorts of codes of behaviour and best practice, encompassing sporting ethics, safety and conservation.

The Doom-Mongers

Anybody new to goose shooting could be forgiven for thinking that there has been a catastrophic decline in standards of behaviour over recent years. Read any book about wildfowling published since the Second World War, and you will invariably find the author complaining that 'it's all ruined now'. The chief accusations normally include overcrowding, excessive bags, firing inappropriate weapons at idiotic ranges and commercial greed. It makes for depressing reading.

In the introduction to a new edition of *Tide's Ending*, published in 1980, BB makes this lament for the halcyon days:

> With the construction of new, fast motorways and the increase in population, many of the great haunts of wildfowl where I enjoyed much sport between the wars are now overrun with what are termed 'marsh cowboys' – irresponsible shooters from the industrial cities, armed with pump guns and even rifles, who fire at anything that flies. On one particular estuary, I saw them sniping at roosting geese from the sea wall with the consequence that the wildfowl deserted the area and are now finding sanctuary on the big estates inland, only flighting out to sea when in need of grit and a 'wash and brush up'.
>
> Another more sinister factor is the introduction, each winter, of parties of foreigners, mostly Italians and French who, like the 'cowboys', slaughter every bird they can, including gulls. In some areas, wildfowl clubs have restricted this indiscriminate shooting on the foreshore, but their policing is difficult to enforce since the laws relating to shooting below high water are still extremely vague.
>
> I am only grateful that I knew the sport of wildfowling at its very best, that is, in the years preceding the Second World War and a short time after. Then, the lonely wastes of the Wash were thronged with fowl in the winter – great battalions of pinkfeet coming in at dawn with barely a shot fired at them.

This makes grim reading for today's generation of goose shooters, and it is supported by many other contemporary accounts. Yet where have we heard this sort of complaint before? From none other than Colonel Peter Hawker! In *Instructions To Young Sportsmen* the Colonel fulminates:

> The average of shooting, on the coast, is now far inferior to that in many private rivers and ponds, by reason, that, where the wildfowl contribute to the winter subsistence of the fisherman, they are for ever followed, and not only by them, but every vagrant, who can raise a few shillings to purchase an old musket; so that, on their appearing in numbers, there is generally assembled a levy en masse, who, by indiscriminately firing at all distances . . .

And so he goes on, in vintage Hawker style. He was for ever ranting about the 'idle, drunken, mischievous rabble', and he was, of course, referring to the situation in the early nineteenth century. What are we to believe? In *The History of Wildfowling*, John Marchington points out that for wildfowlers of the nineteenth century transport was a major problem. As a result, coastal areas within reach of large populations were doubtless overshot and those in out-of-the-way spots were not.

The situation in the first half of this century was probably not quite as

48

idyllic as it was made out to be either. For example, not many miles along the Norfolk coast from the Wash, at Wells-next-the-Sea, geese were present in vast numbers up until the inter-war period, and then the shooting pressure began to take its toll. In *Norfolk Fowler*, published in 1953, Alan Savory recounts:

> There were countless geese wintering at Wells during the 1920s. I have heard it said that there were 20,000 at times. You could sum up the personality of Wells as a mixture of salt winds, pine trees and wild geese. It was the Mecca of the wildfowler, and almost world-famous . . .
>
> In the end, it was overdone. A morning flight at Holkham was a thing to avoid. There were shooters behind every tree, and hidden all along the sandhills. When the geese did come over, everybody fired. But the great birds stuck it out, until some people, who should have known better, started digging-in on the sandbanks where the geese roosted at night, and 'plastering' them by moonlight. That finished it, as no amount of shooting on the banks and the gap could ever have done. That and the ploughing up of the fresh marshes during the war, and the battle school, and the planes!

So the problems of overshooting and disturbance are hardly new. But is the situation today as bad as the doom-mongers make out? I am convinced that the *general* standards of behaviour have actually improved greatly since BB's day. It is interesting to note that the geese have now returned to north Norfolk. The massive growth in wildfowling clubs which police large tracts of the foreshore, vastly improved legal protection, a plethora of wildfowl refuges, the demise of market gunning and the vastly improved education of wildfowlers means that the geese are much better protected today, even if there are more goose shooters than ever before. And remember, there are many more geese around today than there were in BB's day. This may be partly due to changes in agricultural practice, but at the same time we should not forget that some gunners of the inter-war and immediate post war years simply shot far too many geese in relation to the goose populations of the time.

Although fowlers have used goose decoys for many years, the popularity of shooting geese on their inland feeding areas over decoys, often organised on a fee-paying basis, is a relatively new phenomenon. There have undoubtedly been some excesses which caused disquiet among the whole shooting fraternity, a situation which seems to have reached its nadir in the early 1990s. In 1993 the respected and outspoken shooting writer, John Humphreys, wrote an article in *The Shooting Times* entitled 'The Killing Fields'. In it he lambasted the commercialism and greed that he felt was infecting certain aspects of inland goose shooting, citing instances of behaviour which disgusted him and had also attracted hostile publicity. Judging by the reaction to his article, it seems that he spoke for the silent majority of goose shooters, who were sickened by the behaviour of an unrepresentative few.

As a consequence of what came to be known as the Killing Fields controversy, the air was cleared and the few rogues left in no doubt that their activities would no longer be tolerated by the responsible shooting community. Another benefit of the row was the revision and widespread implementation of the BASC's code of practice for inland goose shooting, together with its registered goose guide scheme, which we shall examine later.

The Decoy Dilemma

One of the chief concerns about decoying is the shooting of excessive bags. There is nothing new in this. For example, the International Wildfowl Inquiry's report on the status of wildfowl in Scotland, published in 1939, recorded deep concerns about the activities of an unscrupulous market gunner operating in the Carse of Gowrie, who set out stuffed birds or tethered living ones as decoys, and then 'browned' into the settled mass of decoyed geese with a punt gun. The real objection here seems to have been the size of the bag and the indiscriminate method of shooting, rather than the use of decoys itself.

However, mud sticks, and many authorities labelled decoying as unsporting. Some of the criticism was ludicrously ignorant. For example, in *The Grey Geese Call,* Bill Powell records that one Member of Parliament, talking during the debate on the 1954 Wild Bird Protection Bill, likened the use of decoys to that of sniping at soldiers trying to rescue wounded comrades! The MP concerned claimed to 'know a little of this business'. As Bill Powell could not resist commenting, 'Surely "little" is the operative word!'. Bill Powell himself disapproved of shooting geese on their feeding grounds, although for rather more logical reasons.

When did inland decoying become respectable? For some, it never did. In *The New Wildfowler,* published under the auspices of the BASC, Noel Sedgwick dismissed decoying: 'This method has sometimes been made much of by "romantic" writers, but, while stalking feeding alert geese may well prove to be an arduous undertaking, shooting them over decoys, by daylight, or when they feed under a bright moon is quite infra dig.' This comment was left unchanged in the third edition, published in 1989, by which time inland goose decoying was being widely practised by many gunners, including a large number of BASC members who considered themselves to be both ethical and conservation-minded. It is also interesting to note the favourable attitude to stalking geese.

More than a decade earlier, in *The Practical Wildfowler* (1977), John Marchington explained the wildfowling establishment's ethical objections to decoying as follows:

> Firstly, it is not difficult to shoot geese, sometimes in large numbers, over their feeding grounds, and nothing is sporting if it is too easy. Secondly, with the enormous growth in the numbers of wildfowlers, if the harassment of geese at both their resting and feeding areas continued then, at the best, the geese would have been driven to winter elsewhere.

A few pages later, he goes on to castigate poor Douglas McDougall:

> In the context of shooting geese over their feeding areas, a book published a few years ago, and given much publicity, is unfortunate. Entitled *Goose Fever*, it narrates the various goose shooting experiences of the author. His enthusiasm and tenacity are undoubted, but most of his shooting is done at geese over their feeding grounds. It may be that the farmers required protection, but the book does not say so, and the newcomer to the sport could gain the impression that the author's behaviour is normal and proper at any time, and anywhere. It is not, and it would be a good thing if future editions of the book said so.

Now John Marchington is an acknowledged authority on wildfowling who obviously cares deeply about geese, so his opinions deserve great respect. But in the final analysis, that is what they are – opinions, rather than fact. I am not sure how firmly decoying was established in the mid-1970s – I was still at school – but it may be that he was indulging in wishful thinking, rather than reporting a truly widespread view. Whatever the situation then, decoying geese on their feeding grounds is now generally accepted by a great many shooters as a thoroughly ethical tactic provided that certain rules are obeyed. Foremost among these is that you should exercise restraint in the number of geese shot. Once again, this is the nub of the matter.

Bag Limits

So what is a sensible bag limit? The tide of opinion seems to be flowing in favour of ever lower limits. In November 1924, according to James Wentworth Day, a Lincolnshire farmer equipped with a 12-bore *and cartridges loaded with AA shot* (my italics) accounted for 44 geese over decoys set on a potato field. It seems that the only reason he stopped was that he ran out of cartridges. This event took place over just three hours, and was apparently lauded in some circles as a magnificent achievement!

In his biography of Kenzie Thorpe, the famous Wash wildfowler and guide, Colin Willock noted that in his best year, 1951, Kenzie had accounted for 414 geese (presumably mainly pinkfeet). Today, it is unthinkable that any one person would even want to bag that many in a season. But if the total number seems excessive, the proportion of the population is even more so. As Colin Willock points out, Kenzie's share of the pinkfoot population in that single year was an astonishing 1.5 per cent! Given the 1994 census figure of 266,000 pinkfeet, that same percentage of today's British wintering population would translate into a truly horrific annual bag of nearly 4,000! Of course, this is a rather spurious hypothetical exercise, but it does make a point about individual bag limits and relative shooting pressures in what were supposed to be 'the good old days'.

In *Tide's Ending*, BB gently chides:

> Two gunners shot 13 geese on Portsollen tip on the morning flight. They were using decoys. But the sight of the bundle of big orange bills and brown heads tied together by the neck, the limp, plump bodies with wings awry, piled on the stone floor of our fowling quarters, filled me with sorrow. Most wildfowlers want one good day at geese, I have done so myself, but once you have shot more than eight geese at one flight the joy has gone.

Even eight geese sounds rather too many by today's standards, and in talking about his own 'one good day' I believe BB was referring to an occasion when he shot nine at a single flight over decoys. To his credit, however, he was far ahead of his time in condemning large bags, and in this he never wavered.

Douglas McDougall, who was a shooting pal of BB's, recounts in *Goose Fever* how he once shot 17 geese to his own gun during a single flight (in 1955). Thereafter he set himself a limit of six geese per flight, which he exceeded on one or two occasions as he saw fit. By the standards of his time, he was probably rather restrained.

This is more than could be said of Peter Scott and a friend one night. In *Morning Flight* he records how he and a companion once bagged 80 pinkfeet between them (12 were captured alive, of which nine survived and were kept in captivity). They were shooting inland under the moon. Admittedly, as soon as Scott realised how far matters had gone he expressed remorse. He said that he had published the details as a warning to fellow wildfowlers.

I once shot five geese within a few minutes – three pinkfeet and two greylags – before unloading my gun and watching the birds stream over me for the next 40 minutes or so. I do not like to guess how many I could have shot on that remarkable occasion, but I stopped because five seemed like a lot. I suspect that had this occurred several decades ago, my fellow shooters might have scoffed at my unease, but as it was I felt slightly embarrassed. How would Kenzie have reacted if he had been guiding me?

Today, few people would criticise anyone for shooting two geese, and three or perhaps even four geese might be acceptable – particularly after a few blank flights. Shoot any more, however, and you would certainly attract the disapproval of many other fowlers. In the 1989 edition of *The New Wildfowler*, Eric Begbie suggests an individual limit of three geese per flight, while James Douglas, in *The Sporting Gun,* believes that nobody can justify more than two birds per flight. Furthermore, he says it is a good discipline to include in this limit any geese that you have hit but not bagged.

This matter of where to draw the line is far from clear-cut. What was acceptable yesterday is not acceptable today, but where will it all end? In an age where shooting 400 woodpigeon over decoys is applauded both as a sporting achievement and a feat of pest control, we should not be too hard on our forefathers.

Stalking and Driving

Stalking involves creeping up on geese as they feed or rest, while driving entails somebody putting the geese up in such a way as to make them fly over concealed gunners.

BB was fond of a good stalk, and as I said earlier even *The New Wildfowler* seemed to have some sympathy with this practice. Bill Powell seems to have thought that stalking was perfectly acceptable. I find this slightly puzzling, because it is obvious to me that virtually all stalks will take place on the feeding grounds, with feeding geese as the quarry. Perhaps the explanation lies in the fact that it is unlikely that many geese will be bagged from a stalk, whereas the apparent ease of making of excessive bags is the underlying objection to decoying. Today, the general feeling seems to be that stalking feeding geese is acceptable, but only in circumstances which do not cause general disruption or harassment. In effect, this seems to mean stalking only small groups, and even then only within a short time after the birds have landed on the fields in the morning.

As for driving, this seems to be subject to the same constraints. It is most likely to happen when a party combines stalking with trying to send the geese over one or two static guns, or when birds have landed too far from the decoys and are put into the air in the hope that they will fly over the concealed guns. Be warned, however, that driving geese too frequently will almost certainly earn you black looks from other fowlers.

Skybusting

An evil which all responsible goose shooters deplore is what the Americans call 'skybusting', which means shooting at geese which are clearly out of range. Obviously, this is liable to cause unacceptable rates of wounding, in addition to unnecessary disturbance. This is an area where all the evidence tells us that the average modern gunner is much better behaved than his predecessor. Egged on by the wildly inflated claims of certain gunmakers, and unconstrained by any laws or even etiquette restricting the use of inappropriate weapons such as rifles, many early gunners did indeed blaze away at all ranges. Naturally, this sort of behaviour was much more common on the foreshore than inland, for the simple reason that the general public had much greater unrestricted access to the foreshore, and the geese generally fly higher there.

We still have a few fools in our midst, of course, but most wildfowlers are not prepared to let them get away with it for very long – especially not in this media-intensive era, where outrage and scandal are the currency of ratings. Convention has now set much more realistic ranges for sporting shotguns, and the average goose shooter of today is much better informed about the practical performance of various gun/cartridge combinations and methods for calculating range. If nothing else, skybusters can no longer hide behind the excuse of ignorance.

Foreshore vs Inland

The foreshore purists sometimes sneer that decoying is too easy, claiming that 'one goose bagged on the foreshore is worth three bagged inland'. Occasionally, circumstances combine to make decoying very effective (or easy?) and then the goose shooter who truly respects his quarry will limit his bag. But in the main, inland decoying is a fine test of the skills of concealment, fieldcraft, tactics and knowledge of the quarry, to say nothing of marksmanship. Bagging a goose on the foreshore is indeed a notable achievement, particularly today, but success here may depend as much on luck as on skill, so I think the smugness of the foreshore purist is perhaps unjustified. I should add that I have seen more out of range shooting on the foreshore than inland – perhaps through frustration – and it seems likely that a slightly higher proportion of shot geese are lost on the foreshore, for obvious reasons. Nonetheless, I have to admit that the environment below the sea wall has a magical quality which cannot be matched by anything inland.

With the current popularity of goose shooting, it is probably just as well that so many of us choose to go inland. For the best of reasons, the wild-fowling clubs invariably have to restrict their membership, and sometimes the waiting lists effectively deny would-be fowlers the chance to become truly familiar with the foreshore. Where the public right to access for wild-fowling still exists, overcrowding is often acute. Finally, despite the huge increase in goose populations, the changes in their roosting and feeding habits means that today's wildfowler has a relatively slim chance of bagging a goose below the sea wall.

For the generalist coastal wildfowler, who is chiefly interested in duck, the occasional opportunity of a goose comes as a welcome bonus. But the single-minded goose enthusiast will naturally be drawn to the places where most of the geese are, and this means inland.

The Sacred Roost

Harassment is another hotly debated subject. The general opinion currently seems to be that although it is legitimate (with due restraint) to shoot geese on their feeding grounds, they must never be shot on their roost. The ratio-nale for this is that geese have a wide choice of ground to feed on (although they have favourite fields), so as long as they are allowed to feed in peace for most of the day, no great harm is done. The roosts, however, must never be disturbed, because this will certainly drive the geese away. Not only are suit-able roosting sites much more restricted than feeding grounds, but shooting them in the growing darkness of evening may cause untold disruption and confusion among family groups of geese, as well as destroying their much-needed sanctuary.

One can, of course, shoot geese flighting off the roost at dawn, as long as one is far enough away from the sacred ground. Some believe that it is also permissible to flight geese going back to the roost, provided that they are intercepted some way from it. This cannot be less ethical than shoot-ing them at dawn flight, with two important caveats: first, geese going back to roost often fly in just a few big skeins, so the disturbance factor of shoot-ing may be greater; and secondly, the gathering darkness makes it more difficult to mark and retrieve fallen birds. Ideally, you should have a dog, and ensure that you are in open ground. Wasting shot birds, or allowing a wounded goose to escape and perhaps suffer without taking proper pre-cautions and making strenuous efforts to retrieve it, are very grave breaches of etiquette.

Wounding

It was an incident with an irretrievable wounded goose that made Peter Scott finally decide to give up shooting. In *The Eye of the Wind*, he describes how a single goose flew over a party of gunners – including Scott – and a total of 12 barrels were fired at it. The goose was hit and came down on an inaccessible mudflat, badly wounded and immobile. Later that same day Scott noticed that it was still alive, as it was the next day. For him, this was a defining moment, coalescing other doubts that had gradually emerged.

He still paid tribute to the good things about wildfowling, saying:

> I had derived enormous pleasure, good health and interest from being out on the marshes at dawn and dusk. The birds with their beauty and wildness had been an endless source of delight. The difficulty of outwitting them, the discomforts and occasional dangers – these, and not the killing, made the sport of wildfowling one of the most exciting in the world.

Every wildfowler will appreciate these sentiments, which give the lie to the abolitionists' propaganda about 'blood lust'. For Scott, however, the balance had been tipped too far.

Sometimes I wonder how 12 barrels failed to do the job. Was the goose out of range? And why did they not have a dog if they were so close to the mudflats? Yet this is quibbling, because we have to accept that wounding does occur in shooting. Have we a right to inflict such suffering in the course of an enjoyable pursuit? Few people believe there is any suffering involved in a clean kill, but what about wounding? I admit that I sometimes have qualms when I fail to kill a goose cleanly. Scott recognised that, in the end, it is a matter of personal conscience, and he did not simply turn his back on wildfowlers, saying: 'Perhaps so long as man is deriving so much good to offset the bad, the balance might still fall in favour of the wildfowler.'

How much suffering does wounding cause a goose? I do not suppose we shall ever really know, but some evidence suggests that lightly wounded birds, at any rate, recover very rapidly. In this context, I think we give the general public entirely the wrong idea when we talk of 'crippling'; lightly wounded geese certainly are not crippled in the normal sense of the word, and we really should use a more appropriate term.

I recall that a companion of mine captured a wing-tipped greylag. We were shooting with Alan Murray, who had a collection of geese in his garden. Within three days, our formerly wild goose was happily taking corn from the ground at our feet along with the other birds, showing no signs of fear, let alone stress or pain.

X-ray examinations of geese carried out years ago showed that about 40 per cent of the adults of the two main quarry species – pinkfeet and greylags – carried one or more pellets. Most of these birds would have taken several years to accumulate this shot, of course, and in general they do not seem to have suffered any long-term ill-effects, with most being in good condition. Nonetheless, it is a disquieting statistic, although there is some evidence that the proportion of birds carrying shot today is lower than it was then. I am not certain why these birds were not suffering from lead poisoning, but I can only reiterate that the researchers judged them to be in generally good condition and of normal weight.

A common remark of the anti-shooting brigade is: 'How would you feel if you were shot?' Well, I happen to have an inkling. In June 1982 I commanded a platoon of Scots Guards at the battle of Tumbledown Mountain, in the Falklands. After a good deal of fairly vicious close-quarter fighting during the night, we overran the enemy position with fixed bayonets. While we were mopping-up at the summit of the mountain, a band of the retreating enemy ambushed us, wounding three.

There is of course no valid analogy to be drawn between combat and wildfowling, but my experience of being shot may illustrate something about the mechanism of suffering. I am not entirely sure what hit me; it seemed to be a combination of splinters from some sort of explosive device – a rifle grenade or mine – and fragments from machine-gun bullets which had struck the rocks around me. But the effect must have been much like being hit by a gigantic shotgun, as I was liberally sprayed with shards of metal. Most hit my legs, although one complete round went straight through my right bicep, fortunately being deflected from my chest by the stock of my rifle. No major organ, bone or blood vessel was badly damaged.

I can recall vividly the horror of seeing the tracer flashing all around me, but being unable to react fast enough. There was a momentary burning sensation as the bullet went through my upper right arm, and my rifle was wrenched away as if by an angry giant. A split second later I was bowled over by an enormous, numbing blow across my thighs, which knocked me several yards. It was as if somebody had hit my legs with a side-swung sledge hammer. We were in open ground, and the enemy continued to fire at us.

At first, I thought I had merely been hit by the debris thrown up by the bullet strikes. On my count of three, another soldier and I got up and literally sprinted 20 or 30 yards towards cover as the rounds crackled all around us. My right leg suddenly gave way under me, and when I put my hand down to grip my thigh, my fingers went in up to the knuckle. Only then did I realise that I had been hit by something more substantial than peat and gravel. Many hours later, while being carried out, we were mortared by the enemy and many of the stretcher bearers were killed or injured. I had a few more bits of metal in me to add to my considerable collection. Despite this, a comrade and I staggered, crawled and slid our way to the medical post, a good ½ mile away.

Now, the salient points are these. First, I felt no pain at all when I was actually shot, just an enormous blow and a numbing sensation. Indeed, I felt no real pain for many hours, and I did not bother to give myself morphine, even though I was carrying plenty. Admittedly, the pain did eventually arrive, but it was never particularly intense. Secondly, despite being blasted by about 30 fragments, I was able to move quickly at first, after the initial shock. Later, when my wounds had stiffened, I was still able to cover ½ a mile (albeit with assistance). Of course, I would have become unconscious and died from loss of blood if my wounds had not been bound with field dressings, but it would not have been a particularly painful death. Lastly, the will to survive proved to be incredibly powerful, and many of my actions were driven by instinct.

It was a very frightening and distressing experience, and if I thought that a wounded goose felt the same, I would give up shooting tomorrow. Yet I am confident that this is not the case. In my predicament, I understood exactly what was happening to me; I was wounded, I no longer had a weapon, the enemy were still trying to kill me, they were initially only 50 or 60 yards away, we had just caused them heavy casualties – I could work out the implications for myself!

In short, the physical pain was relatively insignificant; the real distress was caused by mental anguish, a consequence of an ability to think, imagine and reason which is immeasurably greater than that of a goose, which may be only slightly more frightened by a gunshot than by a farmhand crossing the field.

Appropriate Weapons

Having said this, we should of course do all we can to minimise the chance of wounding geese. In this context, I am bemused by the way in which some people automatically decry the use of big-bore guns inland. As we shall see, the 12-bore is very suitable for goose shooting at moderate range, while the big-bores, if correctly handled, may be effective at slightly greater range. What is wrong with that? Presumably, some people overestimate the effectiveness of the big guns and fire them beyond the range of both their own ability and the capability of the load. But this is the fault of the individual shooter, not the gun, and applies equally to 12-bores. At the other extreme, being under-gunned for geese is as silly as using a trout leader for salmon fishing.

Those opposed to big guns seem slightly confused; some say the big guns are too effective, others say they are too cumbersome to be effective! They cannot have it both ways. I believe that a big-bore is more likely to result in a clean kill at reasonable range, especially where one is obliged to use ballistically inferior non-toxic alternatives to lead shot.

The prejudice against semi-automatic and pump-action shotguns is slightly more understandable, if equally flawed. After all, some of these weapons featured in the worst excesses of the 'Killing Fields' episode, and I suppose the semi-automatic 10-bore magnum could be portrayed as the epitome of over-the-top firepower. Somehow, repeating weapons have connotations of combat, which is alien to our sporting traditions.

The intrinsic safety of these weapons is no worse than any other type, but because the action cannot be broken open for all to see, there is perhaps a slightly greater chance of operator error. Furthermore, they tend to have non-automatic safety catches.

Safety

It is all too easy to forget that most safely catches are no more than trigger locks. Given a sufficient jolt or jar, a gun may still go off even if the safety is on. It is partly for this reason that I do not like the way some people appear to think that merely breaking a conventional shotgun but leaving the cartridges in it is safe. Not only is this rather illogical, given that the purpose of opening the breech is ostensibly to show that the chambers are *empty*, but if the shooter trips the barrels might snap shut just as the gun is jarred . . .

There is some debate over when the safety catch should be taken off in taking a shot. Many believe that the only correct way is to slide it off *as* the gun is mounted to fire. Personally, I think this is an overcomplicated procedure, and I am further put off by an unpleasant experience many years ago. I was lent a friend's old 16-bore at an informal clay-pigeon shoot. This gun had not been serviced for many years and had developed the unholy combination of a hair-trigger and a stiff safety on the top strap. As I attempted to slide the safety forward, with my finger on or near the trigger, my whole hand tightened, with the result that the wretched gun went off. Naturally, I was pointing it in a safe direction, but I was in no doubt whatsoever about the enormity of my crime. Ever since, I (like many others) prefer to move the safety catch a second or two before mounting the gun, and only then do I place my finger anywhere near the trigger (I lay it alongside the guard until just before I shoot). I believe this is acceptable.

Given the uncertain nature of safety catches, you should *never* leave a loaded gun unattended in a hide or along a hedge, nor should you stand it up against a fence or leave it in a position where it could topple. I dread to think of the number of times I have seen a boisterous labrador trample all over a gun laid down in a hide, its claws clattering audibly all over the triggers and guard.

As for hammer guns, I love them dearly but I have no illusions; they require even more care than modern guns. For a start, watch out for the hammers getting caught in camouflage netting and cocking themselves. Also, you should be very careful about cocking and decocking the hammers, especially when your hands are cold. The better guns either have an under-lever or allow one to move the top lever across and break them before letting the hammers down, but some have to be decocked before being broken.

The Bagged Goose

Another important consideration is the care of a goose once it has been shot. Obviously, if it has not been killed outright, then it should be dispatched immediately. The best way to do this is to grab it by the legs in one hand, tuck the wings under your arm, and place two fingers of your other hand underneath its chin, with the thumb on top just behind the skull. Then, after extending the neck as much as you can, quickly twist the bird's head back and up, pivoting around your thumb and dislocating the neck with a distinct 'give'. With a really big greylag or Canada, you may find it better to put the head on the ground under your boot, pulling the legs upwards with both hands. An alternative method is to hold the goose by the neck just below the head and twirl its heavy body round until the same thing occurs, but this is very unsightly and messy. Whichever method you use, the bird will move involuntarily for a few moments after the neck is dislocated, but death is mercifully quick. I hate killing wounded geese by hand, and nowadays I tend to use a humane dispatcher – a tool similar to a pair of pliers, which breaks the bird's neck quickly and cleanly. You can buy these implements from dealers who supply poultry and game-rearing equipment. The one problem is that the necks of big greylags tend to be too big for the gape of the jaws.

Never leave a runner until the end of a flight. Not only is this callous, but you may well lose it when it recovers from the initial shock. Geese can run and swim with remarkable agility. When you walk up to a downed goose, always carry a gun and have a supply of cartridges in your pocket. Better still, send a dog. The bird may only be stunned, and could suddenly run, or even fly. Nothing is more ludicrous than puffing across a field in pursuit of a wounded goose.

When shooting, if you hit a goose hard but it stays in the air, or if you notice one which somebody else has hit hard but not brought down, then you should fire at it and continue to do so until the job is finished – *on no account should you simply switch to another target.* This is the only occasion on which it is acceptable to fire beyond normal range.

Once you have collected your goose, you should still treat it with respect, as befits a worthy quarry and a potential meal. I am dismayed at the way people who should know better sometimes throw dead geese into the back of a vehicle in an untidy jumble, to be sat upon by dogs and crushed into odd shapes by various bric-a-brac. You should fold the head under one wing, punt-gunner style, and smooth the wings to the body. Once you have arrived at your base, lay the bird down on its back on a cold floor for a few hours until the body heat has dissipated, then hang it carefully by the neck in a cool, fly-proof room.

The Code of Practice

Now we come to the BASC's Code of Practice for Sporting Agents and Guides Offering Inland Goose Shooting, to give it its full title. This is endorsed by Scottish Natural Heritage, the Scottish Landowners' Federation, the National Farmers' Union of Scotland and the Association of Chief Police Officers (Scotland). This in itself is significant, in that it clearly identifies Scotland as the place where the code was originally needed, and it puts the onus for controlling behaviour on the commercial guides and agents. However, we can take it that the code sets out the standards for acceptable behaviour in *all* goose shooting, for *all* participants. I should point out that the code is subject to annual review and possible revision, so you should check with the BASC at the start of each season to see if there are any detailed changes, especially in the bag limits.

The code has 11 guidance points. We shall examine each in turn.

1. Goose shooting is a traditional and highly valued recreation for many people. If carried out responsibly it brings sustainable economic benefits to rural areas and helps prevent damage to crops.

2. Agents and guides must make their clients aware of the law concerning goose shooting, in particular that:

a) it is illegal to use a semi-automatic or repeating shotgun with a magazine capacity of more than two cartridges for shooting geese or other wildfowl.

This means that one could load a total of three cartridges in a repeater – one in the chamber and two in the magazine. Before crying that three is too many, stop to think how many of us try hastily to reload another one or even two cartridges into a conventional gun when we get the chance after a shot!

b) it is illegal to use a tape recording to attract geese for shooting.

It is also illegal to use a mechanically propelled vehicle or boat, or an aircraft in immediate pursuit of any wild bird for the purpose of 'driving, taking or killing'. Nor may an artificial light be used, except to help retrieve a wounded bird. In 1981 the law also prohibited the use of night-vision devices.

c) it is illegal to sell, exchange or barter wild geese or any part of them (only sufficient birds should be shot to satisfy the requirements of the shooters or their friends).

d) the shooting of ducks and geese in Scotland on a Sunday is prohibited.

e) the penalty for (a) and (b) above is £5,000 (maximum), the penalty for (c) is a fine of £500 (maximum), and the penalty for (d) is £1,000 (maximum).

3. Putting out food to attract geese for shooting is completely unacceptable and those responsible for shooting parties must ensure that farmers on whose land they shoot do not do so.

Most of us can see the sense of this, but how many of us cheerfully feed up flight ponds for wild duck? Yet we have to accept that geese deserve special treatment.

4. There should be no more than eight Guns in a shooting party, which must be supervised by at least one experienced guide who has been properly briefed as to his responsibilities. Safety must be paramount at all times.

My personal opinion is that eight is too many. I have discussed this with many guides and listened to their arguments, and I can see the commercial considerations. I think four is an ideal number, or six at a stretch. Trying to conceal and control eight people is difficult, and apart from anything else it is most unlikely that they will all get a fair share of the shooting.

5. Those responsible for shooting parties must instruct clients in range judgement before taking them out and stop out-of-range shooting immediately, if it is observed. Extra guides must be provided to ensure adequate supervision of inexperienced Guns.

Deer stalkers have a tradition of asking untried clients to prove their accuracy by shooting at an 'iron stag' near the cottage before going out onto the hill. I used to wonder if an 'iron goose' would be a good idea, allowing fowlers to acquaint themselves with the sight picture of an average-sized goose in relation to their gun barrels. Then I read a history of the Morecambe Bay Wildfowlers Association and discovered that they have been using an iron goose mounted on a pole for many years! As a rough guide, when the outspread wings of a goose appear to overlap the muzzles of a 28-inch barrelled 12-bore, the bird is within 40 yards. One of the most annoying problems with decoying occurs when either a novice or a greedy fool fires too soon, ruining everybody else's chance and possibly merely wounding the goose.

6. Shot size one or three are widely considered the best for goose shooting at a normal maximum range of 30 metres. However, experienced Guns may use shot sizes BB or four in suitable circumstances. Every effort should be made to minimise wounding and to retrieve all shot birds.

Thirty metres is just under 33 yards, which may seem much too close. Yet this is a longish shot for a 12-bore against a goose, and even longer for the shooter. I took careful note of the distances at which driven pheasants were actually shot (as opposed to shot at) over a season, and the average range on our fairly typical shoot was certainly less than 25 yards! Bill Powell used to advise people not to shoot at a goose unless it was within 35 yards, on the basis that it was almost certainly further away. To novices, a goose at 30 yards looks as close as a mallard at 15. I think the 30-metre figure may be a bit too restrictive in practice, given the distance at which one normally has to set decoys, but it is not a bad way of trying to impose the realities of effective range on potential skybusters.

On the issue of retrieving wounded geese, it seems to me that there are still too many fowlers without dogs, or even ready access to somebody else's.

Another issue is the use of non-toxic shot. You will need to keep yourself up to date with the current situation, but lead shot is not supposed to be used in 12-bores (other bores to follow in due course) where the shot is likely to fall into wetlands. According to guidance issued by the UK Lead Poisoning Working Group, the definition of wetlands is 'estuaries, salt marshes, foreshore, lakes, reservoirs, gravel pits, ponds, rivers, marshes and seasonally flooded land (river flood plains, water meadows, and grazing marshes) where it would pose a significant threat of poisoning to wildfowl'.

7. Those responsible must provide instructions on the identification of quarry and protected species and provide adequate supervision while shooting is taking place. It is illegal even to shoot at some goose species.

The main problem here is probably Greenland whitefronts in Scotland. Remember, you must not shoot at *any* whitefront north of the border. If you inadvertently shoot a bean goose out of a skein of pinkfeet, most fowlers would understand – although the law might not. In this context, the law seems to have been poorly drafted, as it seems more likely to penalise innocent shooters than protect an abundant species which is an uncommon visitor to Britain.

8. Generally, geese feed by day and roost at night on water or on large open areas. Excessive disturbance can cause geese to desert traditional roosts and feeding grounds: it is therefore preferable to shoot them on the flight lines between roosting and feeding areas.

Note the word 'preferable'. Everybody knows that inland decoying largely involves shooting geese on or very near their feeding grounds.

9. Shooting geese leaving their roost in the morning causes less disturbance than shooting them when they return in the evening. Shooting should not take place at inland roosts more than once a fortnight.

Many of us think that shooting should *never* take place at or too near roosts.

10. Geese must not be harried all day. Shooting should generally stop two hours after sunrise and the ground be left undisturbed for the rest of the day.

Here the principle is sound, although in practice geese seldom stick rigidly to a fixed routine. Particularly when they have been flighting under the moon, they may delay their morning flight until well after dawn, so it may be a little too restrictive to pronounce a cut-off after precisely two hours. On the other hand, decoys should certainly not be sat over long into the late morning, let alone the afternoon. The geese must be allowed to gain proper sustenance without wasting too much valuable energy and therefore losing condition.

On the subject of condition, true wildfowlers will exercise voluntary restraint when snow and ice make life difficult for the birds, in advance of any statutory hard-weather suspension of wildfowl shooting.

11. A bag limit of five pinkfeet or three greylag per Gun per shooting session should be observed. Because of possible changes in goose populations, bag limits may be altered from season to season.

This is probably the most contentious part of the entire code. Many goose shooters think these bag limits are simply too high. For example, eight Guns could bag a total of 40 pinkfeet at one flight, and still fall within the code, even though most fowlers would say this is excessive. Depending on interpretation (and opportunity), a group could conceivably combine the bag limits of the two species to get a totally unacceptable figure of 64!

The important thing is to treat the bag limits as indicative and a force for moderation when exceptional circumstances occur, rather than as targets. In trout fishing, a two brace limit all too often becomes a two brace 'target', with anglers thinking that they should expect – even have the right – to take two brace. It would be a sad day if goose shooters start to hide behind the letter of a law or code, as opposed to acting within the constraints of conscience and custom.

George Reiger provides a vivid example of how even the tightest regulations can have the opposite of the desired effect. In *The Wildfowler's Quest*, he describes the scene at a private shoot in South Dakota:

> The setting was magnificent but the pass shooting was mechanical and verged on slaughter.
>
> Despite a one-goose daily limit designed to enhance the hunting experience and to reduce shooting pressure, brigades of expectant hunters were fed into trenches overlooking the reservoir. All guns fired on one whistle signal and were silenced on the next. Each shooter then grabbed a goose – any goose would do – and hightailed it for the opposite end of the trench where trucks waited to take the first fire teams back to the farmhouse where other platoons of shooters were waiting to fill the trenches. Each pulse of shots sounded more like an execution than hunting. One trench might serve a hundred shooters a morning. Canadas flighting off Oahe were enduring the equivalent of assembly-line slaughter and some of the most intense shooting pressure anywhere in North America.

As so often, it takes an outsider to point out the unique and favourable aspects of British practice. Reiger was very favourably impressed with our traditions of self-regulation, pointing out, 'American hunters are always asking themselves, "is this or that *legal?*" while British sportsmen ask whether or not it is *right.*'

One of the features of our system is that it depends, in the end, on achieving a broad consensus based on reasoned argument and practical common sense. We want individual fowlers to take responsibility for their own actions, based on a sound understanding of the underlying issues, rather than hiding behind codes of conduct or even statutes of law. We cannot afford to become too rigid in interpreting codes of behaviour or we will undermine the solidarity of the wildfowling community while providing ammunition for our enemies. While we all know it is sometimes a fine line to draw, most of us instinctively know when it has been crossed.

Reiger concluded his chapter on Britain on a slightly ominous note:

> I pray the British never take their sporting traditions for granted and permit wildfowling to deteriorate into the pathetic game of 'cops and hunters' it too often seems in the States. There may always be an England, but will there always be the grand unfettered sport of British wildfowling?

CHAPTER FOUR

Shot Sizes and Loads

B e warned! A discussion among goose shooters about the best shot size is likely to provoke heated debate. This is an area where controversy reigns. Hard facts are difficult to come by, yet everybody seems to be quite sure that their own pet theory has a unique force of reason.

In very broad terms, the debate has two main protagonists: the heavy brigade, whose members have a hard core of traditionalists determined to defend the honour of big shot such as BB, and the upstart light brigade, equally convinced of the merits of number three shot and its ilk. The heavy brigade accuse their opponents of relying on drawing-board theory to the exclusion of practical experience in the field, while the light brigade retort that the heavies are clinging to unsound custom. In recent years, the light brigade have been very much in the ascendancy, although the issue of non-toxic shot – which we shall consider later – has thrown up an entirely new area of uncertainty and argument.

What both sides can agree on, however, is the importance of shot size (in reality, shot performance). Given this, together with the fact that a gun is no more than a mechanism for delivering a load of shot, it seems entirely appropriate that we should look at the vexed question of shot size and load before we discuss guns. Shot is, after all, what kills the goose. Goose shoot-ing is a great deal more than just a means of harvesting geese, however, and all ethical sportsmen wish to kill their quarry as cleanly as possible, mini-mising any chances of wounding. At the same time, we do not want the carcass to be so riddled with shot or otherwise damaged as to be inedible, nor do we want to face an unreasonable restriction in range.

The Requirement

Tradition has it that geese are both incredibly tough and exceptionally wary birds – two undeniable facts which, when combined with the size of the goose in comparison with more familiar gamebirds, seem to call for large doses of heavy shot. Geese are encased in a thick layer of feathers and down, a tough skin, and a layer of fat. Great sheaths of muscle, as befits a powerful migratory bird, lie over the sternum, which in turn acts as a shield protecting the goose's vital organs. All this means that killing an 8 lb (3.6 kg) goose cleanly at a range of perhaps 30 or 35 yards is a very different proposition to killing a 3 lb (1.36 kg) pheasant at 20 or 25 yards. But *how* different?

The mechanism of lethality is still not entirely understood. In essence, however, it seems that enough pellets of shot need to penetrate far enough and with enough force to cause lethal damage to the tissues and organs of the bird. More specifically, the damage has to 'switch off' the brain. Anything which halts the supply of blood to the brain, or disrupts the nervous system sufficiently, will do the job. There is some debate over the effect of shock, but we shall return to this later.

A key factor in the ability of a pellet to cause damage is its striking energy, which is traditionally measured in foot pounds. Striking energy is largely a function of mass and velocity, with heavier, faster pellets having more strik-ing energy than lighter, slower ones.

But striking energy is not the whole story. Theoretically, a pellet the size of a cricket ball might weigh the same as a much smaller pellet. If both struck a bale of hay with the same velocity (and therefore much the same striking energy), the smaller pellet would penetrate much further because its strik-ing energy is contained within a much smaller area of presentation. An indication of the penetrative capabilities of a pellet is given by its energy density.

For maximum efficiency, the pellets should impart maximum shocking power as they penetrate. Animal cells are largely composed of liquid, mainly water. Water is incompressible, so a severe blow to a trapped body of water may cause it to rupture its containing vessel, causing further damage. In this way, a high-velocity projectile may cause considerable damage to the tissues some distance from its path. In some extreme cases, this 'hydrodynamic shock' effect may be considerable, especially when the projectile is penetrating dense tissue. However, driving pellets or bullets at extreme velocity may actually be counter-productive if the projectile deforms too rapidly, as that will limit penetration. This tendency for fast, soft bullets to 'blow up' without penetrating properly is well known among big-game hunters.

Yet by comparison with most rifle bullets, shotgun pellets travel at relatively low velocity, and birds in general are much less dense than most land animals. This means that shotgun pellets cause relatively little damage to tissue beyond the acutal wound channel and there is little evidence that pellets deform in soft tissue.

Given adequate penetration and striking energy, there needs to be enough pellets to strike the goose, so that one or more causes sufficient damage in the right place to ensure a swift death. This is not just a question of the number of pellets, but also ensuring that they are spaced in as even a pattern as possible, thus maximising the efficiency of a given load of shot. We shall examine pattern *quality* in the next chapter, because the boring of a gun barrel has much to do with this aspect. Pattern *density*, however, is related at the most basic level to the size and nature of the load. The two issues are closely related, but you should remember that in practice the densest pattern may well be less lethal than one which is less dense but more uniform.

Small shot gives a dense pattern, but may be deficient in striking energy and penetration. Large shot, on the other hand, may have more than enough striking energy and penetration, but there may be too few pellets in the load to ensure that vital organs are hit. Over-large shot may kill the odd bird at extreme range by chance, but all too often it will cause unnecessary wounding at anything beyond moderate range. A bigger load of large shot can be used to gain more strikes, but there are practical limits to what a gun – and the shooter – can fire accurately and safely.

Using pellets which are too small could conceivably smash geese at short ranges, where it results in far too many strikes, while it will do little more than prick the birds at longer ranges. Trying to speed up the smaller pellets, to give them enough striking energy, may result in an uneven or 'blown' pattern, as well as excessive recoil – and perhaps even dangerous breech pressures in your gun.

As with many things in life, the best solution is a matter of compromise and balance. The problems lie in deciding how much striking energy, how much penetration, and how dense and even a pattern you need. This is where the root of all the argument lies.

Clean Kills

Before discussing these considerations further, let me make one thing quite clear: I strongly believe that we should attempt to kill a goose cleanly, by which I mean quickly and with the minimum distress to the bird. A certain amount of wounding is, sadly, inevitable in shooting, but I think that pulling the trigger when you know you are likely to wound is unethical. In short, I do not think it is justifiable to use a gun with the prime objective of simply *bringing down* a goose. I may be unfairly maligning a minority of the heavy brigade, but I have a feeling that some people use very large shot on the grounds that if even one of the huge pellets hits the goose at almost any range it will bring the bird down. This is a misguided view, if not actually callous.

Not that the light brigade's approach should be taken to extremes, either. Quite apart from the problem of pricking, a pellet which is too small could conceivably penetrate to a goose's heart if fired at close range, but the very small wound channel could result in the bird flying on for many hundreds of yards without apparent injury, before dropping from loss of blood. A larger pellet might have caused enough damage and trauma to have stopped the heart beating, causing instant death.

There is room for debate over what we mean by a clean kill. The important issue is the degree of suffering, if any. A goose which is hard hit and brought to bag almost immediately may be acceptable, though a more rapid kill is very much more so.

Conventional wisdom has it that a shotgun load kills by a combination of shock and damage to vital organs. My own experience leads me to believe that the role of shock in shotgun lethality has been overstated. I am not saying that shock never kills, nor that it is not useful in contributing to a clean kill, only that it should not be relied upon. Shock may kill a goose, although more often, it will stun it, and perhaps even drop it. But I believe that the overwhelming majority of geese that I have seen shot *dead in the air* were hit by at least one pellet in a vital area – by which I mean the brain, heart, spine or neck. Other acceptably quick deaths – within a few tens of seconds – may have been caused by pellets striking the lungs with considerable force, or severing major blood vessels at the top of the heart or causing massive haemorrhaging of the blood-rich liver. These are all methods of switching off the brain.

It is worth clarifying what we mean by shock in this context. Essentially, there are three types of potentially lethal shock: we have already referred to hydrodynamic shock, caused by the stress wave associated with a projectile passing rapidly through dense tissue; next, there is hypovolemic shock, where the rapid loss of blood may cause organs to stop functioning; lastly, neurological shock – an overloading of the nervous system – may cause cardiac disruption. All three categories of shock may occur together, but the important issue is that none kill geese as consistently as the direct physical disruption of vital tissue by the pellet.

Note that I said 'dead in the air'. To some extent, this is a matter of perception. It is, I suppose, entirely possible to stun a goose so that it falls heavily from a great height and is killed on impact with the ground – especially if this is frozen.

I believe that many shooters have little real idea of how many pellets have hit a bagged bird, or where they struck. Unless one carefully plucks and examines a carcass, one can be misled by spots of blood on the feathers. On one occasion when somebody triumphantly displayed a partridge 'killed purely by shock' I was able to show them how the pellets had in fact passed straight through the bird, leaving tell-tale blue pin-prick holes on either side of the body cavity. The resistance offered by different parts of a bird's body varies enormously; away from the sternum and the main flight muscles, there is little to stop a pellet passing straight through, and this seems to be a much commoner occurrence than many shooters realise. Indeed, American researchers examining mallard shot at 40 yards found that only one-third of the birds retained any pellets at all.

Many shot geese seem to have broken wings when they are picked up. Sometimes shooters attribute this to the effect of large shot. Yet if one calculates the chances of hitting a wingbone fair and square with shot (even the smallest sizes), they seem much too remote to account for the regularity of broken wings. I think the reason may be a combination of fragility and impact damage. A goose's wingbone is under great stress, especially when the bird is using maximum power in an effort to escape. The bone's structure is a compromise between strength and rigidity. Even a slight nick by a pellet could result in a fracture as the bird beats its wing, in the same way as a carbon fibre fly rod may suddenly snap at a place where it has been scored by a sharp object. Game shooters have occasionally witnessed birds flying on after being hit, and then suddenly collapsing in mid-air with a broken wing. In addition, I think that many wing breaks are caused when a shot goose crashes to the ground. Compared with pheasants and other gamebirds, geese have much longer wings, which are therefore more vulnerable to damage when the bird is out of control.

In *The Grey Geese Call*, Bill Powell illustrated the case for using BB by recounting how he once shot a goose which flew on for a mile before collapsing. On examination, the dead bird proved to have an enormous wound in its side, presumably caused by the impact of several pellets which had fused together – a phenomenon known as 'balling'. He took this as confirmation that geese are extraordinarily tough and should be shot with large pellets like BB.

Reluctant as I am to disagree with such a distinguished authority, I have to say that I draw a very different conclusion from his story – namely, that no matter how large a pellet you use, it will not kill cleanly unless it hits a vital organ; shock alone does not necessarily kill cleanly.

In *Goose Fever*, Douglas McDougall mentions that of a sample of live geese fluoroscoped in 1953, one was carrying nine BB pellets, two had .22 bullets, and one had a .303 bullet in its abdomen! The BB pellets may well have been picked up over several incidents, and it is just possible that the bullets were virtually spent when they hit the geese. Nonetheless, even a spent .303 bullet has considerable striking energy (or could the goose have eaten it?).

Anyone who has shot rabbits with a .22 rimfire rifle will know that unless the animal is hit in the brain, neck, spine or thorax, it will not be stopped immediately. Yet the striking energy of a standard-velocity 37.5 grain hollow-nosed .22 bullet at 50 yards is 77 foot pounds. For comparison, a BB pellet fired at standard velocity has a striking force of a little over 6.5 foot pounds at the same range. In other words, the .22 bullet has a striking energy equivalent to nearly a dozen BB pellets (not to mention vastly more efficient transferral of energy) but, if it is not placed correctly, it will not stop a soft-skinned 3½ lb rabbit! What, then, is the likelihood of stopping a heavily muscled greylag weighing twice as much with a few BB pellets in a non-vital area? Bill Powell has inadvertently given us the answer. So much for shock.

In *Fowling For Duck*, Mike Swan recounts how he shot a mallard which, after initially faltering, recovered and flew on for more than 200 yards before collapsing. On examination, this duck proved to have been hit by no less than 14 number seven pellets, of which 11 had struck the body. Two pellets had passed clean through, two had hit the lungs and one had pierced the heart. Significantly, none had hit the head, neck or spine. He says: 'Since then I have taken to much closer examination of my bag in relation to whether they fell dead or wounded, and have come to the conclusion that birds which literally collapse in the air and fall dead invariably carry a pellet or two in the head, neck or upper spine.' I have come to much the same conclusion, although I believe that pellets causing enough damage to the heart, lungs, liver or major blood vessels may also cause a death that is quick enough to be counted as a clean kill.

Mike Swan also remembers an incident when he shot a Canada at about 30 yards, firing 1¼ oz of number one shot. The bird fell but was retrieved alive by a dog, and dispatched humanely. When plucked, the bird proved to have been struck by about a dozen pellets, several of which had passed straight through. None had hit a truly vital area.

A Deeper Look At Penetration And Striking Energy

How much striking energy and penetration does a pellet need to reach the vital organs of a goose? According to the data in the *Eley Shooter's Diary*, large birds, presumably geese, should be cleanly killed by about four pellets each of a minimum of 1.5 foot pounds striking energy. Medium-sized birds, such as grouse or pheasants, should require about three pellets of .85 foot pounds.

In order to see what this means in practice, we can examine Sir Ralph Payne-Gallwey's experiments, which he published in 1913 in a pamphlet entitled *High Pheasants in Theory and Practice*. This is an account of his amazingly Heath Robinson experiments, which involved suspending freshly killed pheasants on kites at predetermined heights, firing shotguns at them, and then carefully recording the results. There is some evidence to suggest that live tissue has a different level of resistance to shot from dead tissue, but I understand that in the case of Sir Ralph's experiments the practical difference was likely to be negligible. Modern researchers have looked at penetration by using Nato standard 20 per cent ballistic gelatine as a tissue substitute, but while the unnatural uniformity of this material is fine for comparing different pellets and materials, it cannot replicate the real thing.

Using number six shot driven at standard velocity, Sir Ralph fired many shots and recorded results which, while perhaps not entirely scientifically valid by today's exacting standards, clearly suggested that pellets with 1.4 foot pounds of striking energy were only just sufficient to kill a pheasant cleanly. This corresponds to the performance of a number six lead pellet at about 40 yards (or at least that of the pellets at the front end of the shot string). This accords with general game shooting experience, but the significant point is that this minimum value of striking energy is far beyond the stipulated minimum for a pheasant – indeed, 1.4 foot pounds is nearly equivalent to the recommended individual pellet striking energy for a goose, let alone a mere pheasant! So what is the implication of this for the recommended minimum striking energy for a goose? American tests carried out in 1968 at Patuxent Wildlife Research Centre showed that a pellet required a 'threshold energy' of about 0.5 foot pounds just to penetrate the feathers and skin of a mallard.

It seems likely that an odd pellet will always find an especially easy route through the body, although this is likely to be through non-vital areas. In order to be reasonably certain of a clean kill, we require a pellet which is capable of penetrating a goose's sternum or skull, and that is a much tougher proposition than penetrating the abdomen.

In *8-Bore Ammunition*, Douglas McDougall works on the basis of 1.7 foot pounds for geese. He seems to base this on the fact that a goose is approximately twice the weight of a pheasant, and the Eley data specifies a minimum of .85 foot pounds for a pheasant.

However, I feel that the basis of his calculation is flawed. First, as we have seen, it seems clear that .85 foot pounds may be insufficient as a 'safe' minimum for a pheasant; the realistic figure is much more than this. Secondly, although a goose is indeed about twice the weight and size of a pheasant, a pellet may need more than twice the energy in order to penetrate twice as far. Thirdly, a goose's vital organs are very much more heavily protected.

So, to summarise, a pheasant may require to be struck in the right place by a pellet with a force of considerably more than .85 foot pounds – perhaps as much as 1.4 foot pounds – whereas to kill a goose cleanly and consistently the pellet may have to penetrate twice as far (which may be more than twice as difficult) through tissue which is anyway much tougher than in a pheasant. In this context, 1.7 foot pounds seems inadequate – it leaves far too much to chance.

G T Garwood, known to generations of shooters as 'Gough Thomas', mentions in *Gough Thomas's Gun Book* that a correspondent had carried out a number of experiments which indicated that a minimum figure of 3 foot pounds would be more appropriate for geese. In *The New Wildfowler in the 1970s*, Gough Thomas recommends 3 foot pounds for the larger geese, such as Canadas, and 2 foot pounds for the smaller ones. I agree that 3 foot pounds may be taken as the 'safe' figure.

Some authorities produce calculations which include phrases like 'punch factor', where the total of the striking energy of a load delivered on target is measured. In my view, this may be misleading, because below a certain threshold of striking energy and penetration *all* pellets are non-lethal, no matter how many of them are delivered on target. This sort of cumulative calculation tends to overstate the lethality of certain non-toxic shot loads, which may deliver more strikes than their lead equivalents but with a reduced penetrative capability per individual pellet.

Pattern Density

No matter how much striking energy a pellet has, it counts for little unless it hits a vital area. If we accept that 3 foot pounds is the minimum 'safe' striking energy we require, then what is the minimum 'safe' pattern density? It has been accepted by many authorities that an average of 70 strikes in a 30 in (76.2 cm) diameter circle should be sufficient for a goose.

Wild geese have very different proportions to farmyard geese, or to familiar ducks such as mallard. The chief distinction is that wild geese have much larger wings in relation to the rest of their body; they look bigger than they really are. I recently measured the area of the underside of a reasonably large (thought not abnormal) greylag. This bird had a wingspan of 60 in (152.4 cm), and with wings fully extended as if flying presented a total flat area (one surface only) of about 440 sq in (2,838 sq cm). This looks like a very large target.

But then I measured the proportion of this area which comprised the vital areas, such as the brain (as opposed to the entire head), neck and upper chest cavity. This area totalled just 36 square inches (154.8 sq cm)! By comparison, the largest surface of a standard clay pigeon accounts for about 14 sq in (90.3 sq cm).

The total area encompassed by a 30 in (76.2 cm) circle is slightly more than 700 sq in (4,561.6 sq cm, to be exact) so a perfectly regular pattern of 70 pellet strikes within the circle should result in one pellet for every 10 sq in (64.5 sq cm), which equates to roughly 3.6 pellets in the vital area of my goose. A little light for the shock theory, but we have already discounted that. The fact is that a single pellet in this tightly defined vital area could kill, and there is evidence to suggest that single-pellet kills (not to be confused with single pellet strikes) are indeed much more common than many people realise.

However, once again we ought to veer on the side of safety. For a start, no shotgun pattern is anything like perfectly regular (especially if the pellets have been blasted through a high degree of choke). Furthermore, a considerable part of my delimited vital area was occupied by the goose's lungs, and a pellet here may not achieve the truly instant kill we are after. Nor would the simple pellet counts be consistent – we could easily have variations of 5–10 per cent in this factor alone. In addition, a smaller goose, such as a pinkfoot, would present a much smaller vital area, as would any goose flying at an angle. Then we have to give some leeway for aiming errors and the fact that many pellets at the tail of the shot string do not achieve the stated striking energy. Lastly, the shot string effect means that no moving target will receive as many strikes as a static pattern plate. Gough Thomas seemed to favour a minimum of 80 strikes, so we shall work with this figure.

Finding a Balanced Load

This leaves us with a relatively clear task: we need to find a balanced load that will deliver a minimum of 80 strikes in the 30 in circle at a minimum striking energy of 3 foot pounds. I shall assume, for the moment, that we are talking about lead pellets.

The heavy brigade's beloved BB retains adequate striking energy right

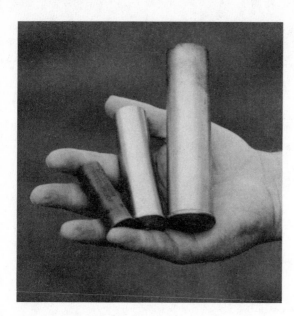

Big Bores can carry huge amounts of shot. Shown are 2-bore and 4-bore brass cases in comparison with a 12-bore cartridge.

out to nearly 90 yards, which is a long shot, even for a punt-gun. As for the light brigade's champion, number three shot dips below the magic number at 45 yards, which is about the accepted maximum range for a 12-bore. Number one shot should be good for about 65 yards.

There are 70 pellets of BB to the ounce, 100 of number one, and 140 of number three. Assuming we have a gun which throws a true full-choke pattern at extended range (a rather uncommon occurrence, incidentally), a heavy 12-bore load of 1½ oz of BB shot will run out of pattern density at a mere 33 yards! Number one does better, running out to a bit beyond 42 yards, while number three romps home with about 51 yards. As far as most 12-bore loads are concerned, the light brigade seem to win the argument.

Moving up to big bores we find that number one shot comes into its own, giving a suitable density right out to nearly 65 yards with 3 oz. BB only begins to make the grade in a whopping 4 oz load, and even then the pattern fails at about 67 yards.

I should say that I have seen a great many geese killed stone dead by 12-bore cartridges loaded with BB. Having faith in one's cartridges is a notable advantage in shooting, just as a favourite fly is an aid to confidence in fishing. But an examination of the facts in the cold, clear light of scrupulous objectivity shows that, in most circumstances, BB is out-performed by lighter shot.

All too often, I suspect, gunners who believe in BB fail to make the necessary distinction between the number of geese they *bring down* and the number they *kill cleanly*. Most practical loads of BB will kill geese very effectively at short and moderate ranges, and are also capable of killing geese at prodigious range – but only if a lucky pellet happens to strike the right place. This characteristic may give BB's supporters an entirely false idea of its true capabilities. More often, however, BB fired accurately (and that is another story!) at long range is overwhelmingly likely to wound, rather than to kill cleanly. In contrast, number three shot will kill cleanly right to the very limit of normal 12-bore range, while number one shot is effective at even greater ranges.

At the opposite end of the scale, a friend of mine shoots geese over decoys with 1¼ oz of number four shot fired from an ancient 12-bore game gun, choked improved cylinder and half. He is absolutely deadly with this combination, although he never shoots at a range of more than about 35 yards. At this range, the pattern density is probably better than 125, while the pellets retain a striking energy of around 3.08 foot pounds. This is perfectly adequate. He is sensible enough to pass up the many opportunities which are offered at longer ranges. The salient point is that the limiting factor for his cartridges – striking energy – runs out at around the same range as the limiting factor for a heavy 1½ oz load of BB, which is pattern density.

The fallacy about the 'knock down' capability of exceptionally large shot at extreme range has been illustrated in the case of duck by research carried out in America by the Department of Game and Fisheries. In these experiments, 2,010 mallard were shot in flight from the side by an electrically fired gun at a variety of ranges. Two sizes of lead shot were used, equating to our number five (a widely recommended size for mallard) and number three (as favoured for duck by some of the heavy brigade). The gun was a heavily choked 12-bore firing 1¼ oz commercial loads.

At 30 yards, both number five and number three shot were instantly effective on 95 per cent of duck. At 40 yards, however, number five scored 71 per cent, overtaking number three which scored 66 per cent. At the extreme range of 60 yards, the superiority of the smaller shot was even more evident, scoring 24 per cent as opposed to 18 per cent. It should be noted, incidentally, that these last figures are far too low to justify taking a shot, as a clean kill becomes a matter of mere chance, as both pattern and penetration are largely inadequate at this range. If a heavy load, fired through a full-choke barrel with optimum timing and perfect accuracy, can only score a clean kill once every four or five times at this range, then what chance do you or I have?

However, the large-shot brigade might glean some momentary comfort from the result of a much smaller number of shots fired at the duck head-on at 50 yards, where number three shot seemed to have the edge over number five. The explanation is probably that at this angle the duck's vital organs are much better shielded, so that although the larger pellets were less likely to hit the target, they were more likely to be effective on the few occasions when they did. But in any case the overall scores for both sizes of shot were very low at this range and angle.

Recommended Shot Sizes

Considering all the evidence, my own choice of lead pellet size (all other factors being equal) would be as follows: for small-bore guns and 12-bore loads up to 1¼ oz, number four, though with a strict range limit of 35 yards for the heaviest loads, and even less for the others; for all other 12-bore loads, right up to 2 oz, number three; for big-bores, right up to the 4 oz four-bore load, number one. I would not use BB in anything smaller than a punt-gun.

Earlier I indicated that shotgun pellets are much less efficient at transferring their striking energy than rifle bullets. This is largely because the sphere is such an inefficient shape for a projectile. The relatively high ratio of surface area to mass causes a shotgun pellet to slow down much more rapidly than a bullet, which means that it loses its striking energy much more quickly. In addition, on reaching the target a well-designed bullet will deform in a controlled manner, spreading but retaining virtually all of its mass, and so doing maximum damage. A shotgun pellet, on the other hand, cannot be designed with a hollow point, or a soft nose.

A soft lead pellet will deform more easily than one which has been hardened by a coating or the addition of a substance like antimony. Yet hard shot has the advantage of being more resistant to the effects of pressure and abrasion as it is propelled down the gun barrel, which means that it is more likely to retain its shape and weight, leading to tighter and more even patterns. Tighter patterns can also be achieved by using plastic shotcups instead of fibre wads, sometimes in conjunction with special fillings which 'buffer' the shot, allowing individual pellets a better chance of retaining their shape, velocity and striking energy.

Some people set great store by high-velocity loads, which are supposed to have much improved striking energy and, as a bonus, are 'faster' to the target, therefore requiring less forward lead. But some of these loads develop high pressures, and even if this does not actually blow the pattern, high pressure is generally not conducive to the formation of really good, even patterns. For one thing, large pellets, such as those generally used in goose shooting, do not always take kindly to being blasted through heavily choked barrels at high speed; they sometimes have a tendency to behave more like solid metal than a fluid mass of spheres. And as for being faster, this normally provides little advantage under normal field shooting conditions, although it may have more relevance to clay shooters. For example, the difference in forward lead between one well-known standard velocity load of number six shot and its high-velocity stablemate, against a bird crossing at 40 mph at a range of 45 yards, works out at a total of 5 in!

The Problem with Lead

Lead is the ideal substance for shotgun pellets. But its relatively high mass, high energy density, easily adjustable hardness, malleability, low melting point and relatively low cost are counterbalanced by another of its special properties: the wretched stuff is toxic!

This is not the place to repeat the tortuous arguments about the restrictions on using lead shot. In any case, most inland goose shooting may continue to take place with lead. The places and circumstances where you should use non-toxic alternatives to lead shot were outlined in Chapter 3, under guidance point 6 of the code. But quick examination of the non-toxic alternatives serves to illustrate just how difficult it is to find a replacement which can come anywhere near replicating lead's performance.

The problems are not just those associated with damage to old guns, or the shortening of effective range, nor even increased costs. In the final analysis, guns can be replaced, getting within a reduced range is a test of increased skill, and few goose shooters find that the cost of ammunition is a major part of their shooting budget, let alone the difference between the cost of lead and the cost of non-toxic alternatives. The real problems are to do with reduced lethality and, consequently, increased wounding rates.

The Problem with Steel

Steel shot (in reality, soft iron) is five times harder and 30 per cent lighter than lead. This means that a steel pellet has a much lower striking energy than its lead counterpart, so it has to be propelled at higher velocity. Yet it also loses its velocity more rapidly than lead shot. When it hits the target, its already below-par striking energy is even less likely to be transmitted to best effect. Its lower energy density means that it will penetrate less than lead. In order to deal with these drawbacks, larger pellets (about two sizes larger) are needed to achieve the equivalent striking energy of lead. Yet bigger pellets mean more open patterns, so more of them are needed. But because of its lightness, steel occupies much more room in the cartridge.

Cartridges which are too long sometimes develop high pressures, and in any case over-long charges of shot may cause poor pattern quality. It is also difficult to fire large pellets at high velocity through tight chokes, because steel, being very hard, does not like being constricted. And so the problems go on.

The upshot is that many steel loads have severely limited lethality in comparison with their lead counterparts. So wounding rates go up. In addition, there are other unhelpful side effects, like the increased risk of ricochets and people breaking their teeth on steel when eating wildfowl and problems with harvesting timber which has steel shot embedded in it.

There are now some much improved steel loads on the market, and the Americans have many years of experience in developing effective steel wildfowling loads. But my own rather limited experience of using steel loads against Canada geese in North America has given me serious reservations about the fundamental capability of steel. A companion and I were shooting from a rather luxurious dug-in 'blind' over decoys set out on a stubble field in Nova Scotia. This was long before non-toxic shot became an issue in Britain, although it was already a statutory requirement in North America. We bought what we thought were standard heavy loads of American number four shot (equivalent to our number three) for our 12-bores.

We had some tremendous opportunities, starting with a flock of Canadas right over us at about 25 yards. I could clearly see the pellets strike, but neither of us seemed to be able to kill the birds cleanly, although our loads should have been more than adequate. Our guide, however, told us we should be using BBs, and blamed our cartridges. Only then did it dawn on us that we were using 'waterfowl' loads, and that this meant steel shot. At 25 yards, steel number three (UK) shot probably has a striking energy little greater than that of lead number five shot at the same range and an energy density similar to lead number six. This simply was not enough against big Canadas. We did not have the stomach to continue the flight, as all we seemed to be capable of doing was wounding birds.

Other Non-Toxic Alternatives

Fortunately there are a number of more viable alternatives on the market now. However, no non-lead alternative has ballistics which can match those of lead. A major drawback is the fact that they are relatively light. For example, the grams per cubic centimetre of various materials is as follows:

Lead: 11.3

Molyshot (pellet): 10.2

Bismuth (4 per cent tin): 9.5

Iron: 7.8

Zinc: 7.0

Bismuth is a fractile material, and some of the original loads suffered from fragmentation due to the shock of firing. This particular problem seems to have been solved by raising the tin content to between 3 and 4 per cent and buffering the loads. Bismuth has had considerable field testing, and performs adequately at moderate ranges. It is certainly better than steel shot, and it can be used in ordinary English game guns. I have not used it on geese, but I have used it very successfully on duck at a flight pond, where ranges were generally fairly short.

Molyshot has been used successfully in Holland, but is not yet widely available here in sizes suitable for geese. It does not seem to have the same shattering problem as bismuth. Meanwhile, the Americans have been testing a very dense tin-bismuth-tungsten composite. Finally, in this country David Taylor has found a way of coating lead shot in a new-age sealant which seems to obviate lead poisoning. No doubt other products will be developed over the years.

The chart (on page 82) shows the calculated penetration into ballistic gelatine of pellets of lead, bismuth and steel in sizes BB, one and three at various ranges. A nominal 'entry energy density' has been subtracted. It is equivalent to the 0.4 foot pounds (0.54 J) striking energy the American researchers found was necessary for number six shot to penetrate the surface of mallard. Of course, this is probably too little for geese, but we have no better figures at the moment, and the real purpose of the chart is to compare relative performance. There would be many other variables under field conditions, of course. At a very rough guess, however, I would say that observation in the field tends to suggest that a penetration on this basis of about 80 mm may be the safe minimum for a goose.

Note: the universal measurement for energy is joules. For all practical purposes, 1 foot pound may be taken to equate to 1.356 joules.

Calculated Performance

Muzzle velocity standardised at 400 m/s, and allowing for 0.1 J/mm2 entry energy density based on .5 foot pounds striking energy threshold.
(*Source – Dave Leeming, Ballistics Group, RMCS Shrivenham*)

Material/shot size		Penetration (mm) into gelatine						
	BB	165	153	142	133	123	115	107
LEAD	1	137	126	116	107	98	90	83
	3	121	110	100	91	83	76	69
	BB	136	126	116	107	98	90	83
BISMUTH	1	113	102	93	84	76	69	63
	3	99	88	78	70	63	56	49
	BB	98	88	78	70	63	56	49
STEEL	1	79	69	61	53	46	39	33
	3	68	58	50	42	36	29	24
		20	25	30	35	40	45	50

Range (m)

Note the relatively inferior performance of steel shot at this velocity.

CHAPTER FIVE

Guns

The greylags lit their afterburners and powered up and away from the decoys as the 12-bores spat fire and lead. Three heavy thumps signalled the toll. Unbending our cramped legs, we stood up in the hide and watched as the clamouring geese headed towards the ruined stone wall at the far boundary of the stubble field. We held our breath as they neared it.

Powerful wings rowed the great birds onwards and upwards through the misty morning air. They were just beginning to level out, at a height of perhaps 60 yards, when a great gout of smoke spurted up from the wall. The fiery column seemed to reach out for the geese, one of which crumpled as though it had flown into a plate glass window. An instant later a tremendous noise reached us – a deep, bone-jarring blast, the sort of sound one might normally associate with a distant volcanic eruption.

As we started to cheer, there was a repeat of the smoke and thunder, and yet another doomed goose fell out of the sky. With the first two shots of his brand new four-bore magnum, Martyn Howard had scored a right-and-left at geese. It was an awesome performance.

The four-bore's maker, Alan Myers, was on hand to witness the devastating debut of his monstrous creation. He permitted himself the type of grin that lit up Dr Frankenstein's face when his monster first sat up on the bench. Then he dampened our elation by pointing out that Martyn had not emerged to take a bow. 'Is he all right?' The cheering faltered, then faded. We watched the wall anxiously. No sign of Martyn. 'If he was on that plough on the other side, he's probably been pile-driven in up to his neck,' somebody joked, but the laughter was nervous.

Then something like a small telegraph pole sticking up from a gorse bush began to move. To our relief, we recognised Martyn at the base of the pole – he was carrying it on his shoulder. He was halfway across the field when more geese appeared in the far distance. 'Get a bloody move on!' bellowed Alan gleefully. Martyn started to puff as he attempted to trot – no easy matter when you are balancing a minor howitzer on your shoulder . . .

That evening the mighty cannon went into action again. We had lined out along a fenceline three fields away from 200 feeding greylags. Martyn was on the far left of the line. The geese eventually lifted when it was virtually dark and headed for their roost on the loch 2 miles away.

There is something particularly exciting about flighting geese like this. Anticipation builds during the long, quiet wait for them to finish feeding. Then, finally, there is a distant, spine-tingling roar of wings as they lift into the wind in unison. Which route will they choose? On this particular evening we got it almost exactly right. The noise of calling geese increased, and we strained our eyes. Suddenly a long, wavering line of geese came into view above a frieze of larch trees, silhouetted against the afterglow. The main group were heading rather too far to our left, but we were in with a chance.

I had just thumbed back the hammers of my eight-bore when there was an enormous, bright orange-yellow flash 80 yards to my right, followed by a thunderclap. The four-bore had spoken. I saw a stricken goose planing down. Another eyeball-searing blast, and the geese wheeled across my front, heading between Alan and me. I was still half blinded by the flash – or at least, that was my excuse for missing with my first barrel. But I folded a goose neatly with my second. Alan brought down another, and then it was all over. I am pleased to say that the geese were back on the field the next morning, where we left them in peace.

Of course, it is not necessary to use a big gun for geese, especially inland. In fact, there can be little doubt that a 12-bore magnum is an altogether more convenient weapon, as we shall see later. Big guns – especially those firing black powder loads – are heavy, clumsy, noisy and dirty. But they are also great fun and, in the right hands, extremely effective. They have to be deployed with a certain amount of discretion and restraint, yet they seem to add another dimension to goose shooting, something to do with tradition; it somehow seems right to use a mighty gun for the noble goose.

Those who say one should use one, familiar gun for all shooting are probably right, especially in this age of variable chokes and long-chambered 12-bores. However, such people are also slightly boring. A big old goose gun has personality and stature – probably even a history. A shooter may shoot a goose with a 12-bore, but it takes a real fowling piece to *slay* one.

Alan Savory, in *Norfolk Fowler*, gives this account of a big gun:

> The eight-bore was a terrific weapon, weighing 14 lb. It fired black powder, and went off with a hollow roar like a signal rocket. The cartridges that I had with it were green and red. Some of them had waxed ends instead of a turn-over, and all were old. The first time that I shot with it, I set fire to the reeds on my friend Jack's inland flighting marsh. A very low mallard came over in the afternoon, just about skimming the alder trees. Jack said, 'Go on; shoot it in front, like a partridge.' I roared off with the eight, the duck flared skywards and the reeds caught on fire from bits of burning paper, and a blast like a blow-lamp from the right barrel. The flame seemed to go all the way up to it and it fell through clouds of billowing smoke. We decided to banish the eight-bore to the shore, in future.

The inimitable James Wentworth Day had an eight-bore christened 'Roaring Emma'. In *The Modern Fowler* he recounts this tale:

> Off went Emma, one, two – 4½ oz of shot, a double sheet of flame, and a roar that could be heard at Salcott.
>
> And the next minute, as Will put it, 'There come a rare scuttlin' and a-rowing, and a blarsphemin' that would ha' scorched a donkey's rudder!' Someone was away in a great hurry. We could hear them rowing away, the tenor of their remarks growing no whit dimmed by distance.
>
> 'Reckon you must ha' hotted up one of those Mersea men,' Will remarked, as we gathered the slain. To a Tollesbury man there is not much difference between a dead curlew and a dead Mersea man, except for the important gastronomic fact that you can at least eat the former with some semblance of enjoyment.
>
> Three months later, in all innocence, I landed on Mersea Hard, with 'Roaring Emma' under my arm. Will stood off in the punt, preserving that proper air of armed neutrality which is natural when visiting foreign waters. A lean, sharp-looking individual with a weather-beaten face, and a sort of Norseman's beak, regarded me with professional curiosity.
>
> 'That's a rare gret ole gun you've got there, master,' he volunteered. 'She'll tiddle em up, I reckon?'
>
> 'She will,' I replied.
>
> 'Weigh a tidy bit, don't she?'
>
> 'Seventeen pounds.'
>
> 'Gawd a-mighty! Let me lift 'er.' He did. Suddenly he wheeled a pair of

quick-lit, suspicious eyes upon me, and shot out: 'Do you be the gentleman wot shoot over at Tollesbury?'

'I do', I answered, still unsuspicious.

'Then you're the b– wot nearly shot me ole mate and me last harvest! And that's the bloody gret gun wot did it, too!'

I begged for further details.

'Me and me mate crep' up in me little ole punt to the Hoyles where there was a herd o' curlew feedin'. We was just a-layin' to 'em, when all of a sudden, orf goo a bloody gret gun t'other side of the mud-horse. Thar near as a life a-copped me mate and me. There was a pound o shot come over me 'ead, and a yard of blew flame come out of the gun with a pair o' ladies' knickers, and a whole bloody *Daily Mail*. Gawd, wot a weepon! That orter be chained up!'

Given this sort of delightful mythology, it is easy to see why so many people believe that they need to use a big gun for geese. As so often, the reasoning is based as much on emotion as on logic, but that is a human reaction, after all.

The Choice of Gauge

As we saw in Chapter 4, the goose shooter needs to use relatively heavy loads of relatively large shot. This has a number of implications for the weapons we might use to handle these loads.

For a start, small-bore shotguns such as the .410 and 28- and 20-bore are not best suited to goose shooting. The tiny cartridges of the .410 and 28-bore, for example, do not handle large shot at all well, and the lightness of the load means that even with number four shot the pattern becomes very patchy at a very short range. Long-chambered .410s tend to produce high breech pressures which, together with the very long shot column, may produce particularly poor patterns with large shot. It is still possible to shoot geese with such light and handy weapons, of course, but opportunities for taking a shot without the overwhelming risk of wounding will be very few and far between. It may be acceptable for someone with a medical condition, but a fit adult using such light guns against geese smacks of flippancy and 'trick' shooting.

With the 20-bore – especially in magnum form – the pattern situation is much improved, although it is worth pointing out that a light 20-bore firing what is effectively no more than a moderate 12-bore load may recoil in a particularly sharp and unpleasant manner. By contrast, a light 12-bore will probably handle the same load rather better, with slightly lower breech pressure and more even patterns, so that is preferable. Nonetheless, if you habitually use a 20-bore for game shooting, are confident that it gives you an advantage in terms of familiarity and accuracy, and do not mind the recoil with heavy loads, then by all means use it. With number four shot and good fieldcraft you should be able to use the light gun to good effect at geese within 30 yards, although you will have to steel yourself to let many other opportunities pass. Of course, this only applies to lead shot loads; when it comes to less ballistically efficient shot, anything less than a fairly long-chambered 12-bore becomes virtually unusable against geese.

The 16-bore is a rather unusual calibre nowadays, and is not much suited to firing goose loads anyway. Most 16-bores have chambers which preclude firing loads which can match those of the long-chambered 20-bore, and in any case 16-bore ammunition is difficult to obtain in many areas. Still, it is a pity that these graceful guns have fallen victim to the march of conformity, by which I mean the ubiquitous 12-bore.

Most geese shot in Britain today are taken with 12-bore in its various guises. As the most popular gauge of sporting shotgun, the 12-bore is also the most developed. The wide range of ammunition gives it great versatility, enabling just one gun to be used for all shooting. One can load up with cartridges with number five shot for an expedition after duck, with half a dozen heavier loads of number three shot in a pocket just in case some geese appear. Even ordinary 12-bore game guns may be able to handle loads of 1½ oz, while the heaviest 12-bore 3 in magnums can fire as much as 2 oz, which was regarded as a light 8-bore load in BB's day.

Indeed, this fact has sounded the death-knell of the old 10-bore, which commonly fired a load of less than 1½ oz. Old black-powder weapons of this gauge are still toted by a few enthusiasts, but they are very different from the modern 3½ in chambered 10-bore magnum, which was developed in America after the eight-bore was outlawed there as part of the move against market gunning. Firing loads of 2–2¼ oz or even (in low-velocity home-loads) 2½ oz, the 10-bore magnum handles the sort of load that used to be the preserve of the eight-bore. A few of these guns found their way to our shores soon after they appeared in America, but their great rise in popularity started in the late 1970s, after Eley stopped making eight-bore cartridges. Now 10-bore magnums are available in a variety of configurations and grades of quality, with cartridges available from at least two manufacturers. They may well experience yet another surge in popularity on the foreshore in this era of non-toxic shot.

The 10-bore magnum lacks the versatility of the 12-bore – one cannot really turn up at a driven shoot with one of these cannons! In addition, some people regard it as slightly 'yobbish', in the slightly illogical way that people do. It lacks the heritage of the eight-bore, which is the traditional heavy fowling gun. The fact that some automatic shotguns are available in 10-bore magnum has served to add a few more prejudices. This is a pity, as it is a devastatingly effective goose gun. Commonly weighing-in at around 11 lb (5 kg), these guns are not so heavy as to be unwieldy, but they fire genuinely heavy loads.

Far more respectable is the prince of traditional fowling pieces, the eight-bore. This really is a wildfowling gauge – it has no other proper application. Eight-bores vary considerably in weight and chamber length, and were usually made to fire black powder, although many have since been nitro-proofed. The shortest chamber length is 3¼ inches, while the longest is normally 4¼ in (although mine has 4½ in chambers). Weights range from about 12 lb (5.4 kg) to over 15 lb (6.8 kg) for the long-chambered magnums, which normally fire loads of up to 3 oz (mine takes 3³⁄₁₆ comfortably, using hand-loaded brass cases).

Some modern eight-bores weigh as little as 9 lb (4.1 kg). This is because they have been made by drilling out modern 10-bore magnums to an internal diameter which barely qualifies as eight gauge. (There is a relatively large range for this gauge, from .835 in to .860 in. Bored out 10-bores tend to have internal diameters of just .803 in to .813 in.) With 3¼ in chambers, these new eight-bores tend to be used to fire the new commercially-manufactured nitro cartridges, which generally have loads of 2½ oz. This is enough to make these guns kick viciously, but of course this load is barely heavier than that of a standard-velocity 10-bore magnum cartridge. Moreover, the light eight-bore is bound to be slightly more fragile than the original 10-bore magnum, so it is difficult to spot any real advantage.

Then we come to the four-bore, which really is a monster. There are single-barrelled four-bores, of course, but even these might weigh in the region of 18 lb (8.2 kg). A double-barrelled version might weigh some 20–25 lb (9.1–11.3 kg), which is getting near the limit of what a strong man can wield.

The traditional 4¼ in four-bore cartridge might pack a load of 3 or 3½ oz, but the modern gun described at the beginning of this chapter has 4½ in cartridges and fires brass cartridge cases holding 4 oz (and could probably cope with a bit more). This means its twin 44-in barrels can hurl a total of ½ lb (227g) of shot into the air at once – a veritable wall of lead. Although nitro-proofed, the preferred propellant for this brute is good old black powder, as it is with so many big guns. It may be smelly, dirty and corrosive, but black powder is also relatively gentle and progressive, propelling heavy loads up long barrels with nice, low pressures. This often results in excellent patterns.

In truth, the double four-bore is barely practical as a shoulder gun. Many were designed to be used as light punt-guns, with both triggers being fired together by means of a lanyard. A tell-tale sign is a hole drilled in the stock, through which the breeching ropes (which enable the gun's recoil to be taken by the boat's forepeak) used to pass.

Finally, we come to the mighty two-bore, which generally fires a whopping 5 oz. Only a very small number of these leviathans have been built for shoulder-gunning use, and they are really more of a novelty than a serious proposition, although I have handled a Myers two-bore which handles better than some eights. All the two-bores that I know of are single-barrelled.

The Most Appropriate Gauge

So which is the most appropriate gauge? The market has already decided that it is the 12-bore, especially in its heavier versions. There is a great deal of sense in this, of course, but I think that the shooter who wishes to take goose shooting really seriously should at least consider a larger gauge. I have to admit that my reasoning is clouded by the emotional appeal of the old fowling pieces, but there is also a hard core of fact, logic and observation in my argument.

The big-bore's disadvantages are probably at their greatest under moon-flighting conditions, but this is hardly a fair test as, for most of us, opportunities for shooting geese under the moon are relatively rare. Instead, let us take normal decoying, which is how most geese are shot and where many say the big gun is totally out of place.

At what range is the average goose shot over decoys? A lot further than one might think, I contend. Decoys normally have to be laid out in a pattern, with the nearest about 20–30 yards away from the shooter's position, which will generally be in some form of cover. Geese tend to avoid flying low over cover, and they usually aim to land on the far side of the decoy pattern, no matter what the wind direction. This means that the optimum point for taking a shot will very often entail a range of at least 30 yards. This is a long shot for a 12-bore, with very little in reserve to compensate for any problems in pattern quality or pellet penetration, let alone aiming errors. Twelve-bores originally came into their own for walked-up and driven game shooting, but remember a high pheasant is at a range of 30 yards, and most driven or walked-up game is shot at much closer range, perhaps 20–25 yards.

In the course of a season's decoying, many geese pass by at a range of about 45 yards, including those which swing over to have a look at the decoys without actually coming in to them. Rather fewer come within 35 yards – they are generally the ones which are actually coming in. On a good day, when they come in great numbers, there will be some at 25 yards, which in practice looks like point-blank range. Many people regard a goose settling into the middle of the decoys as being so close as to be virtually unmissable; then, when they walk out to collect it, they are surprised to pace out the range at a good 35 yards. Taken over an entire season, few geese will ever fly within ordinary game-shooting range of you, unless you're always very well hidden upwind of the decoys and they lift over you as you shoot.

The extra 10 or 15 yards in the range of a heavy 10-bore magnum or eight-bore may seem to be a trifling advantage, vastly outweighed by the disadvantages of increased weight and decreased manoeuvrability. But that extra range is at a distance which is critical, where every extra yard is meaningful and translates into extra opportunities. Furthermore, an eight-bore will certainly throw a much more lethal pattern at 35 yards than a 12-bore. So not only is it possible to hit a goose further out but, at sensible ranges, the big gun may be more likely to result in a clean kill.

Limitations of 12-Bores

I recall a vivid demonstration of the limitations of 12-bores at maximum range during a goose-shooting expedition in eastern Scotland a few years ago. It was my first trip with a certain guide, and there were five of us in the party. Three of us had brought along heavy guns, but the guide kept finding reasons why we could not use them. I suspect that the real reason was that he thought we might attempt to shoot at silly ranges, or before the other members of the group had a fair chance. We shot a few geese over two or three days and then, on the final day, we found ourselves setting up in what seemed to be an ideal position. We had an excellent ditch to hide in, while the decoys were set out with the nearest 35 yards away on stubble. A small party of greylags had been hammering this field for nearly a week. The only problem was the wind, which was blowing along the ditch. We were all equipped with 2¾ in chambered 12-bores, mostly firing moderately heavy loads of number one or number three shot, although one person was using BB.

A pair of greylags materialised from on high, 'whiffled' to lose altitude and came straight in without further ado. As they approached the ground downwind of the decoys and slowed to land, the three people nearest them fired. Both geese were clearly hit. One dropped beyond the decoys, while the other climbed up into the wind and swung over us before anybody within range could reload. It flew on for several hundred yards. To our relief, it then collapsed in mid-air and plummeted to the ground at the far side of the field behind us, where we left it until the end of the flight. Meanwhile, the goose which had fallen beyond the decoys was collected by a dog, and had to be despatched by hand.

Then a singleton came in, dropping well upwind and skimming along 10 feet off the ground for 100 yards as it aimed to settle on the far side of the decoys. Two shots rang out, and on the second the goose crumpled and lay still. A minute or two later we noticed it sitting up with its head raised. It was retrieved by the dog and dealt with.

Later several skeins swirled near, and although none seemed to take more than a passing interest in our decoys, between us we managed to secure another two geese, one of which dropped instantly and stopped flapping within a few seconds, while the other was a strong runner which nearly made it into the air again before being secured by the dog.

One big skein of about 30 birds came over and lost height, to go barrelling along right past us, parallel to the ditch and only 20 yards off the ground but about 50 yards out. We held our fire and hoped they would come round again, but they did not, instead settling in the same field but 150 yards the other side of a hummock.

That signalled the end of the flight, although three geese circled near us just as we were packing up. We crouched down, and those of us who were still loaded fired a few shots, with the result that a single goose came spiralling down. It landed with its head raised, and the dog was sent for it.

As we laid out our haul in a row beside the ditch, I remarked to a friend that it was a pity we had had no option but to let the big skein go. The guide overheard me, and assumed that I was complaining about having to leave the big gun behind. 'There ye are,' he said, holding up a dead goose with a blood-stained chest, 'well shot, right in the chest. Six geese, in difficult conditions, and all with 12-bores. No need for yer big guns at all.'

I did not have the heart to remind him that the goose he was holding had been run down by the dog, and that the blood on its chest came from its mangled wing. Indeed, of the six geese, all shot at ranges of 35–45 yards, only one had been killed truly instantly. Thanks to the dog, none of the birds had suffered, but I still felt uneasy. I am confident that more of those geese would have been killed cleanly had we been using our big guns.

The Role of the Big-Bore

Of course, no amount of shot will make up for deficiencies in accuracy; even an eight-bore will not kill a goose at 35 yards unless a good part of the pattern strikes the bird. Those who decry the use of big guns often make the point that these heavy, cumbersome weapons are almost guaranteed to make anyone shoot below his usual standard, especially if he has had little practice with them. Furthermore, these problems of accuracy, which are supposedly exacerbated by the characteristics of big guns, are even more telling at long range – where the big gun is supposed to be coming into its own!

Like all the best propaganda, there is some truth in this argument, but it is not the whole truth. Human beings come in all shapes and sizes, with varying degrees of strength and physical fitness. I have to admit that I occupy a fair amount of space and it is possibly for this reason that I have no difficulty in wielding a well-balanced 15 lb eight-bore. In fact, my kills to cartridges ratio with this great gun is actually slightly better than I achieve with my custom-made light game gun. Not that we are comparing like with like, of course; the majority of the geese shot with my big gun are technically easy shots – it is only the range which is so much greater than is usual in other types of shooting. Even then, I seldom fire my eight-bore at unwounded geese more than about 45 yards away. One of the things I appreciate about the eight-bore is the way it seems to increase the likelihood of killing a goose cleanly at moderate range. In addition, there is no doubt that a big-bore gun can kill geese cleanly at relatively long range, although I am not for a moment advocating irresponsible skybusting.

There is little doubt that the increased lead needed for long-range shots is a difficult matter to judge. But my personal experience is that the long barrels and greater weight of the big gun give me a much better, smoother swing, which is very helpful in automatically producing longer effective lead. From my point of view, therefore, the big gun is ideally suited to longer-range shooting, and in this I am not alone. I have seen too many right-and-lefts at geese at ranges of up to 50 yards achieved by big-bore shooters to believe that hitting such a large bird at such ranges is technically impossible. I wonder how many geese are wounded by inadequate loads (possibly of non-toxic shot) fired accurately from 12-bores at under 40 yards, compared with those wounded by big-bores fired marginally less accurately at up to 50 yards?

The real problem with big-bores is that some inexperienced shooters may overestimate their performance and behave in a manner which helps to brand other big-bore enthusiasts as irresponsible or greedy. We should be careful not to pander to our own prejudices in this matter, or we shall be on the same slippery slope as the so-called dry fly purists, whose legacy causes ill-feeling on the banks of chalk streams to this day. It is not the inert metal which is to blame – whether fashioned into fishhook or gun – but the person who uses it. In truth the owner of a big-bore is more likely to be a goose-shooting enthusiast, so it follows that he may be more knowledgeable about suitable ranges for geese than the average shooter.

Recommended Gauge

If I was advising somebody on a gun for geese, I would first ask how seriously they were 'hooked'. Someone who habitually shoots with a 12- or 20-bore game gun and wants to shoot a few geese once or twice a year would be advised to use their ordinary gun with a safe, heavy load of number three or four shot (assuming for the moment that it is possible to use lead shot). The same goes for youngsters. A fairly keen wildfowler, on the other hand, may find it best to invest in a 12-bore magnum, which he can use to great effect against geese or ducks, as well as using lighter loads for pigeons and general rough shooting. For those who have really been bitten by the bug, however, I would say at least investigate a modern 10-bore magnum or, if you can afford it, a proper old double eight-bore with long chambers.

You may have to load your own cartridges, of course, but I find that this adds immeasurably to the enjoyment. But whatever you do, check with a reputable gunsmith exactly which loads are safe to use in your gun. You will find several people who can make you brass cases and provide all the kit but, if you do start loading your own, *do not depart one jot from your instructions!* It is obvious that differing loads of shot or charges of powder will cause varying pressures, but so do less obvious variables, like primers, wads, ramming force, cartridge closure strength, the nature of the case material and its fit in the chamber. Do not take anything for granted – ask!

The Question of Choke

Having looked at the options in terms of gauge, this still leaves us with a wide choice in the matters of choke and type of action.

The customary way of obtaining maximum effective range from a shotgun is to constrict the final few inches of the internal bore, creating a 'choke' effect near the muzzle. Full choke gives a relatively tight pattern, while the converse is true of lesser degrees, of which the most commonly used extreme is known as improved cylinder. Most wildfowlers and goose shooters tend to favour relatively heavy degrees of choke because they often have to fire at longer than average ranges, as we have seen. Yet a high degree of choke comes with penalties, in the form of much reduced leeway for aiming errors at moderate ranges, a reduced quality (as opposed to mere density) of pattern and, at short ranges, a propensity to smash birds which may make them inedible.

One of the great advances has been the variable choke which, in its various forms, allows one to select an appropriate degree of choke for a given situation. It is worth noting that it is often possible to fit these variable chokes to guns which were originally manufactured with fixed ones. Perhaps the only real problem with variable chokes is the way they seem to reinforce misconceptions about the certainty of choke performance. All too often, people will talk about the choke of their gun when they have never actually checked it. Unless you have checked the pattern thrown by a particular load in a particular cartridge in your gun, then you have only an inkling of how it performs. For example, plastic one-piece wads may throw a pattern which is considerably tighter than that thrown by traditional fibre wads, while harder shot (especially steel) throws tighter patterns than softer shot. In view of these variables – which may well cause differences greater than the theoretical difference between a full-choke and quarter-choke performance – you will not be able to rely on the choke marked on your gun; you will have to test it yourself.

Twelve-bores are traditionally patterned at 40 yards, whereas Douglas McDougall set the standard for eight-bores at 60 yards, reasoning that each gauge was then being tested at something like its maximum range, which should highlight any serious problems. The problem for the big-gun enthusiast is that there are very few shooting grounds which have oversize pattern plates, or can accommodate a firing point at 60 yards. (Incidentally, the range is from the firing point, not the muzzle of the gun.) But if you have access to a suitable patch of land, you could use the method I adopted in developing loads for my eight-bore.

The key piece of equipment is the pattern plate. Rather than attempting to cope with large plates of heavy steel, I simply bought two 6 feet by 3 feet softwood lattices from a garden centre. If you can get one full-sized 6 feet by 6 feet lattice which folds, so that you can load it into a car, that is even better. I tied my two lattices side-by-side with string, forming a framework 6 feet by 6 feet, and mounted the whole contraption upright on the remains of a fence on a level patch of ground. To record each shot, I placed a piece of thin polythene sheeting six feet square over the framework, using large wooden clothes pegs on each side. My polythene sheeting was cut from a huge roll bought from a builders' merchant, but you could use paper or card, although it is less waterproof and not as easily stowed. I used an indelible felt marker to make an aiming point and also to write the details of each load and barrel in one corner of the sheet. After each shot, I marked the pellet holes (which were easy to see from a slight angle) with crosses and then rolled up the sheet neatly for examination later and pegged up a new sheet.

The firing point was measured out accurately with a rope and a tape measure (do not rely on pacing). Stand at the firing point, aim carefully at the aiming mark (you could use temporary sights) and fire a shot. After marking up and pegging up a new sheet, you repeat this procedure a minimum of 10 times for every load/barrel combination.

When you are evaluating your patterns, you need to spread the sheets out on a large table or on a floor, and use some form of grid which incorporates the standard 30 in circle. I made mine from fencing wire formed into a circle 30 in in diameter with the two cut ends twisted together to form a handle. I then made another perfect circle 10 in in diameter, and bound it centrally within the larger circle by using eight equidistant 'spokes' of thinner wire between the two circles. The result was a grid with nine segments – eight between the two circles and the ninth forming the central circle. This formed a standard pattern evaluation grid.

Place this segmented grid over the pattern marked up on the sheet, judging it by eye so that you achieve the optimum pellet count within the outer circle. Incidentally, I have seen experts advising shooters to fire *at* such a grid drawn on the pattern plate or sheet, but this is clearly incorrect. It takes no account of aiming errors, which are not being measured in this instance. What we are interested in in pattern testing is the number of pellet strikes and the uniformity of their spacing, not their proximity to a notional aiming point.

When you have recorded the number of pellets in each segment, you will have a record of both the total number of hits and their regularity. I always count a pellet which cuts the line as lying within it, and particularly look out for any signs of balling, which would be unwelcome. A variation of about 5–10 per cent within a batch of 10 cartridges is quite normal, although you may wish to discount the occasional pattern which falls well outside the norm as a genuine anomaly.

There are, of course, much more sophisticated methods of evaluating patterns, often involving the use of custom-made software. For example, Dr Roger Giblin, of University College, London, has developed a system which automatically assesses the true centre of the pattern and can give a host of calculations and measurements at the press of a button. A particularly interesting aspect of his work at the Ballistics Research Laboratory was his demonstration of the way three-dimensional shot clouds varied, and the effect this might have on the efficiency of a given load.

The first time I tested the new brass case home loads in my big gun was something of an event. I had been using commercial 3¼ in cartridges, with notably poor results. Not only was the 2½ oz of shot far lower than the gun could handle, but there seemed to be problems with pattern quality and penetration, which may have been caused by poor obturation of these loads in a much longer chamber; some of the hot gasses may have been getting past the wadding. My new brass cases, however, should have solved that problem, and they were all loaded with rather more than 3 oz of number one shot driven by replica black powder called Pyrodex.

I had a *Yellow Pages* directory fastened in the middle of the lattice behind the polythene sheet, because I was also testing penetration in the manner described by Douglas McDougall. I put my ear defenders on. The two onlookers – my five-year-old son and an adult neighbour – moved well back and off to the side. I carefully picked up one of the immense brass cases and clonked it home in the chamber. Then I cranked back the right hammer and squinted down the range at the distant yellow rectangle – and I really do mean distant; if you have never measured it out before, I can assure you that 60 yards looks like an enormously long range for a shotgun, way beyond the normal range of shotgun shooting. The *Yellow Pages* looked tiny. I took aim and pulled the trigger.

There was a shattering crash, a thump of compression against my ear defenders, and 15 lb of heavy artillery thumped back into my shoulder while the 39-inch barrels jumped playfully upwards. A huge cloud of smoke completely obscured the target. Why is it that perceived recoil is always so much worse when you're firing at a static target?

Literally shaken, I opened the gun with an unsteady hand, extracted the hot, smoking cartridge and laid the great weapon on the ground. Bits of card from the wadding column were still fluttering down through the roils of smoke. Taking off my ear defenders, I turned to acknowledge my audience, only to see them hastily scrambling further back. The neighbour asked me over his shoulder if it was supposed to go off like that. I tried to look nonchalant.

After extensive testing to develop the optimum load, I discovered for myself a truism that was noted by Douglas McDougall; at ranges beyond 40 yards, it is almost impossible to achieve theoretical full-choke performance (at least with fibre wadding). The observed reality simply fails to match the theory from the tables, often by as much as 25 per cent. This is yet another reason for erring on the side of caution in designing loads for shooting at maximum sensible range.

Recoil

Recoil is a manifestation of a basic law of physics. All other things being equal, a standard load fired at standard velocity will cause a light gun to recoil more than a similar load fired from a heavier gun, which requires greater force to get it moving. Increasing the velocity increases the kick, as does increasing the weight of the load. (This includes the wadding column and the powder, incidentally. Because it is a relatively heavy and inefficient propellant, black powder may actually result in more recoil than nitro in certain circumstances.)

Over the years, gunmakers appear to have discovered that a weight of charge to weight of gun ratio (assuming standard-velocity loads) of roughly 1 oz (28g) of shot to 6 lb (2.7 kg) of gun is normally acceptable – hence the deliberately heavy weight of an old eight-bore, although some of the single-barrelled versions were notorious for recoil. I believe that BB once had a single-barrelled eight-bore which weighed just 7 lb (3.2 kg) and used to give him a nose bleed when he fired it! Similarly, light 20-bores firing magnum loads may kick unpleasantly, as may lightweight eight-bores, 10-bore magnums and 12-bore magnums. By contrast, heavy eight-bores and four-bores may be more comfortable to fire.

There are various other factors, however, which influence the way we feel recoil. For example, there is some evidence to suggest that the relatively short, sharp shock generated by a fast-burning powder may actually be less noticeable to some people than the same force transmitted more smoothly over a slightly longer time, as might be generated by a slower progressive powder (a fact which runs counter to most taproom logic). Additional factors affecting recoil include the shape of the stock – especially its drop – with straighter stocks seeming to result in lower levels of perceived recoil.

Does excessive recoil really matter to the goose shooter? After all, he will normally be wearing relatively thick clothing, and it is not as though we fire huge numbers of cartridges at a time. Obviously, your gun should not cause you a nose-bleed or make you flinch as you shoot, but assuming that it does not, I am not sure that a healthy shove on the shoulder is much of a problem.

Excessive recoil may help to force a gun 'off the face', and it is often symptomatic of deeper dangers, such as excessive pressures, but within reason it does not seem to bother me much. I have often fired 1½ oz loads from my 6¼ lb (2.8 kg) game gun without even noticing the kick – unless I am firing at a pattern plate where, for some odd reason, it is very notice-able. This seems to be a well-known phenomenon, and illustrates the differ-ence in tolerance to perceived recoil in comparison with actual recoil.

My 15 lb eight-bore kicks a bit with nearly 3¼ oz of shot, though not unduly so. But it did give me a very clear experience of truly excessive recoil one day. I had been testing it for penetration, firing both barrels in sequence in order to save time. The right-hand lock, unknown to me, had a very weak spring. All went well until I altered the firing sequence, firing the left barrel first. When I pulled the trigger, there was a huge explosion and I was con-scious of a very heavy blow to my shoulder and cheekbone; there was a ringing in my ears, and I found I was out of breath. I was not forced back at all, but the gun had very nearly jumped out of my hands. It was all extremely frightening and most unpleasant.

At first I thought the gun had blown up, and there was a certain amount of rather panicky counting of fingers and limbs! Only when I opened the gun did I notice that the initial detonation had jarred the weak right lock sufficiently for the hammer to fall, causing the virtually simultaneous dis-charge of both barrels – a total of about 6½ oz (184 g) – which would not have disgraced a light punt-gun! Although many subsequent tests with empty chambers failed to replicate the double discharge, I had the lock fixed without further ado.

Some people are very susceptible to the effects of recoil, and for them a gun which is relatively heavy for a given load may be the answer. Over-and-unders tend to be heavier than their side-by-side equivalents, and you may see this as an advantage. I am a traditionalist and prefer a side-by-side, no matter what I hear about the OU's narrower sighting plane.

Another possibility is the automatic (technically, semi-automatic, or self-loading). I do not like automatics; to me they seem unbearably ugly, more like combat weapons. I cannot abide all the mechanical clanking, and I find it distinctly off-putting to have an empty case clattering out of the side of the action just as I am lining up for a second shot. On the other hand, the mechanism soaks up a great deal of the recoil force and devotees claim that this results in greater second shot accuracy. And of course, there is the option of a third shot. One notable advantage cited by the Americans is the sheer robustness of these chunky single-barrelled weapons. It is undoubtedly true that they can put up with treatment which would ruin a fine double-barrelled piece.

Another robust mechanism favoured by the Americans is the pump action. Once again, it is not my style, but some people swear by them.

Old fowling authors used to advise against ejectors, as this was just another complicated mechanism which could go wrong under harsh fowling conditions. This consideration may still apply to coastal wildfowlers, but modern ejectors are so reliable that I do not think you should be put off them, unless you load your own cartridges and are worried about losing or damaging ejected cases.

In the final analysis, you should use a gun and cartridge combination which you trust; in the field, faith is worth more than any amount of theory, although I find the latter aids the former.

CHAPTER SIX

Concealment, Clothing and Equipment

As I have said, the ability to get within range of the quarry is the key to successful wildfowling. Wild geese are generally wary birds, accustomed to being hunted by humans and other predators. In order to come to terms with geese in their own environment, one normally has to deploy a considerable range of skills, including those which come under the general heading of 'fieldcraft'. One of the most fundamental aspects of fieldcraft is the ability to remain concealed from the quarry. Another involves the ability to survive – indeed, to be comfortable – in all types of weather. So a shooter's clothing and use of cover to help conceal him from the quarry are closely linked. In particular, both methods involve the use of camouflage.

In the days when National Service was mandatory, many people had the principles of camouflage drummed into them during basic infantry training. More recently, the growth in the popularity of deerstalking has re-kindled an awareness of the same principles, while birdwatchers and wildlife photographers have become adept at the use of sophisticated clothing and equipment. But I would guess that the greatest single contribution to our practical knowledge of camouflage for shooting in recent years has come from pigeon decoying.

The boom in pigeon decoying, and the resultant flood of articles in the sporting press, together with a plethora of books on the subject, has meant that many of today's generation of shooters are familiar with hide-building techniques and what is generally termed 'hide discipline'. Like the wild goose, the wild woodpigeon is a cautious bird, and has even been dubbed 'the wildfowl of the woods'. As a direct result of the education of pigeon shooters – many of whom live in urban or suburban areas – our standards of practice are beginning to approach those of American hunters, who have long displayed considerable expertise and ingenuity in this area, in addition to having access to very good clothing and equipment.

The army trains recruits to understand a number of factors which could cause a concealed soldier to be seen by other humans. The same considerations apply in varying degrees to the conditions we encounter in goose shooting.

Shape

For a start, the shape of a human, if recognised as such, is likely to cause a goose to take avoiding action. It is obvious that they will do this if they suddenly see someone at close range, but it also applies at much greater ranges. It may not be as instantly noticeable, but if a goose sees a person moving around in a field, albeit at a considerable distance, then it is unlikely to fly within range of that spot in the near future. So you need either to wear clothing which breaks up the familiar outline of the human body, or to conceal yourself. Even simply crouching down reduces the probability of your shape being recognised as that of a human, as well as lessening the chance of being seen in the first place. Disruptive pattern material (DPM, to use army jargon) is supposed to do exactly as its name suggests. But the effectiveness of DPM also depends on resolution, which is in turn a factor of range. To give an extreme example, you may walk into a shop and be very impressed with a DPM jacket which seems to mimic woodland leaves in perfect detail. At close range – such as in woodland stalking – this may indeed be very important. But at, say, 300 yards, does it make any difference at all? The details are impossible to see at this range, and it may seem indistinguishable from a jacket of similar overall colour, but no pattern at all. In fact, the only pattern which will still break up the human outline at this sort of range is one with very broad blotches of varying of colour, rather than one with an intricate pattern.

Shine

Shine may either draw a goose's attention to an otherwise concealed gunner or, more likely, simply register as an unfamiliar and unnatural object. In both cases, the effect is much the same – the bird shies away. The chief causes of shine in a goose-shooting situation are gun barrels, followed closely by binocular lenses. Other potential culprits include cameras, watches, flasks and scratched hide poles. But it is not only the sudden flash of these items in the sun which can cause geese to flare. Even non-quarry geese, observed on their Arctic breeding grounds far from the realms of man, show a marked reluctance to fly near pieces of driftwood or flotsam which appear to be incongruous. This suspicion of unfamiliar objects is much increased if they appear to be unnatural. Very few natural objects even gleam, let alone shine. Low-angle winter sunshine glancing off the melting frost on plastic goose decoys will sometimes turn incoming geese at 200 or 300 yards.

Silhouette

The problems of silhouette are sometimes less obvious than others. But someone can be wearing clothing which is non-reflective, with a pattern which disrupts his shape and blends into the background colours, but he will be all too easy to spot if he is silhouetted against the sky or a lighter patch of background. Stalkers are particularly aware of the need to avoid being skylined. One of the most common errors is looking *over* cover, as opposed to *through* or *around* it. For example, a human face peering over a stone wall will tend to be very noticeable, particularly if it is silhouetted. You should always look through a gap, or around a gateway at low level. If you really must look over the top, make sure you do so against a suitable background, such as a tree or bush. For much the same reason, it may be better to site a hide in front of a bank or wall and peer through the netting, rather than automatically taking the more obvious route of hiding behind solid cover and having to show yourself over the top. Having the sun behind you can make you almost impossible to see, but only if you are in front of solid cover and not actually silhouetted.

Colour

The matter of colour is more complex. We assume that geese see things as we do, and we may be right, but how do we know for certain? While goose shooting in eastern Canada, I noticed that the local deer-hunting season had opened. The most obvious manifestation was the hordes of hunters setting off one morning, all wearing their statutory 'blaze' hats and vests. This is a very bright, almost fluorescent orange colour which is worn for safety reasons in the public hunting areas. Some of the vests were blotched in different shades of orange, a sort of highly visible DPM which struck me as faintly comical. I was unwise enough to say so to a local hunter, whose riposte was simply, 'Deer are colour-blind, so as long as the pattern is disruptive, it does not matter much what colour it is.' I was totally silenced! I do not know if deer really are colour-blind, but it set me thinking. So did an article in a shooting magazine, which detailed how a pigeon shooter experimented with various types of hide material. The most spectacular hide was one made of fluorescent orange plastic netting, of the type used to cordon off road repairs. According to the account, it worked splendidly!

Most evidence seems to suggest that geese do have colour vision of a type similar to our own, although they may be able to see certain wavelengths that we cannot. In particular, it seems highly likely that they can detect ultraviolet. This is important, because modern detergents tend to impart UV 'flare' to recently washed clothing. So be careful about washing your favourite goose-shooting outfit.

If we assume that geese do see colours as we do, the important thing is to choose colours which blend into the background. The problem is that we cannot always be sure precisely which sort of natural background we shall have to match, so we inevitably have to compromise. As a general principle, however, the colour of most ostensibly suitable outdoor clothing is too dark. In winter, the sorts of places where we might try to conceal ourselves on the foreshore or in the fields are likely to involve bits of bleached driftwood, dead reeds or rushes, faded long grass, dead leaves, thistle stalks – a blend of ochres, light browns and off-white colours. Against this, the typical dark, mud-coloured thornproof coat stands out starkly. So does a dark green balaclava helmet, unless the wearer is ensconced in a gorse bush. The human face, on the other hand, tends to show up as unnaturally light or pink. It should be covered with something – a face mask, veil, hat or some form of paint or mud on the skin itself.

Movement

Movement is perhaps the greatest giveaway of all. We know how a rabbit may squat among the tussocks in an open field, and only being noticed when it bolts from right under one's feet. Remaining concealed is a complex business involving all the factors we have already examined, but movement can ruin all our hard work in these other areas. Conversely, keeping still can help us to remain unseen, even when we have broken virtually every other rule. Time after time I have been caught in the open by geese, but by keeping absolutely still until the optimum time, I have managed to get a shot.

Having said that geese dislike flying over unfamiliar objects, it is worth remembering that these objects are much more obvious when there are few of them. On their wintering grounds, geese soon become used to round bales, cattle troughs, fences and so forth. This does not mean that they willingly fly near them if they can help it, but if there are a lot of them scattered about, they may have no choice but to overfly some of them from time to time. I have often hidden behind fence posts, and when you occupy as much space as I do, you accept that this as a triumph of hope over physics! The truth is that I have not been 'hidden' at all, but if I remain perfectly still, either I avoid detailed examination or, if I am examined, my inert form is not recognised as something dangerous.

Having examined some of the principles of camouflage, there are three ways of achieving suitable concealment: through clothing, by means of some form of hide, or by a combination of both.

Personal Camouflage

Army snipers seldom bother with any form of hide. They usually wear one-piece suits which can be matched to the specific type of cover, often by attaching appropriate pieces of vegetation or scrim. By remaining very still, they can be virtually impossible to spot, even at point-blank range. But they have a very precise task, which involves firing from a prone position within a very narrow arc of fire. They use rifles rather than shotguns, and often fire at a range of hundreds of yards. This is quite different from a goose-shooting scenario.

American turkey hunters, on the other hand, use shotguns and need to get within close range of their quarry. Like snipers, they also tend to wear highly sophisticated outfits – in this case, made of material which is patterned like tree bark. By sitting up against a tree, they can call a turkey gobbler within range, and then either quickly raise their gun or, in some cases, simply adjust the aim of a gun which is already held by forked branches stuck in the ground. However, this tactic involves shooting at a virtually static target on the ground in a densely wooded area. As with the sniper, the shooting is confined to a carefully defined arc of fire. It is not really appropriate to normal goose shooting.

Some American goose shooters rely solely on camouflage clothing, but this tends to be restricted to certain specialised methods or conditions.

During thick snow, for example, a white suit and strips of non-reflective white tape around the gun barrels may make a shooter practically invisible to the geese. During the decoying of snow geese, where enormous spreads of white decoys – sometimes as many as 1000 in total – cover a considerable area of ground, the geese seem to find it difficult to pick out anomalies, and the American hunters often dress in white snow suits and simply lie out among the decoys, keeping perfectly still.

Sometimes, American goose hunters hide underneath magnum-sized plastic shell decoys, and I know of one person in this country who has tried this method – it worked, apparently, but he never tried it again because it was so uncomfortable. Besides, it curtailed the arc of fire for other members of the party.

Hides

In this country, we tend to use hides for most goose decoying, while relying more on clothing and natural cover for flighting geese inland or on the foreshore.

The purpose of any sort of hide is to provide useful concealment. By this I mean concealment which is effective but still allows us to shoot without unreasonable inconvenience or impediment. If the object were merely concealment, then we would simply dress in a sniper suit and lie down in the best bit of cover. But we want a hide that allows us to intercept the geese at reasonable range, and to shoot efficiently, accurately and safely at flying targets at any reasonable angle within a broad arc of fire. We also need to be able to observe both incoming and departing geese for some distance (not least in case any drop after being shot at) and to see various markers or objects in order to estimate range. Any protection from the weather is welcome, but this is very much a secondary consideration, and is more properly the task of the clothing system. Other considerations include the ease with which a hide can be built or moved, its durability, how easy it is to tailor it to local conditions, its flexibility, cost, size and so forth. In essence, there are two types of hide: natural and artificial.

Natural Hides
The chief advantages of a natural hide are that it normally requires very little work to improve or make habitable, while at the same time it is likely to form an inconspicuous part of the landscape by virtue of the fact that it is natural. On the other hand, it may not be in precisely the right place, nor will it necessarily be entirely suitable for the people and equipment you want to conceal.

The ultimate natural hides are the sort of living willow structures purposely planted and created on some inland marshes for duck shooters. Much more common, however, is a horseshoe bend in a creek winding through saltings, or a pile of seaweed and flotsam. Inland, ditches and the dead grass caught up at the foot of wire fences may provide cover, as do the eroded banks of streams, clumps of gorse, small bushes, stone walls, rocks and so on. It is quite astonishing how adept some people are at making use of natural features to hide themselves. A few minutes with a trenching tool or a brashing knife will enable a skilled hide builder to hide himself with what seems like remarkable ease.

Many early books on wildfowling included detailed descriptions of sand pits, which were generally dug on tidal flats to intercept geese either on or very near their roosting areas. As we have seen, this practice is generally frowned upon today.

An effective method of concealment on bare ground – inland or on the foreshore – is simply to lie flat, with your gun either across your chest or by your side. You will need to raise your head, either by a small, hinged plywood board which can be propped up like a picture frame, or by piling up some earth. You may also throw a camouflage net or loose vegetation over yourself. The chief drawbacks of this method are to do with the fact that it does not really fulfil the functions of a hide: it makes it difficult to see anything, difficult to judge range, difficult to shoot – difficult altogether!

Artificial Hides

The artificial hide – often improved with natural materials – has enormous advantages over most natural hides. The chief of these is that it allows us to hide pretty much where we *want* to, as opposed to where we *have* to. While the nature and terrain of wildfowling below the sea wall tends to favour the use of natural hides by individual shooters, inland goose shooting often entails the use of artificial hides, for two main reasons. First, inland goose habitat often comprises broad, open fields with very little natural cover. Secondly, shooting over decoys usually involves a small party of shooters, all of whom need to be well hidden within a relatively small area. In this situation, adequate natural cover cannot be relied upon.

There are two basic types of artificial hide – permanent and portable. North Americans seem to use permanent artificial hides for goose shooting much more frequently than we do. The most common form is a pit sunk into the ground, with revetted sides. These 'blinds' are sometimes sold in prefabricated kit form, and really sophisticated moulded plastic versions are also available.

In Chapter 4 I mentioned my dismal experience of trying to shoot Canada geese with steel shot in Nova Scotia. The blind we used on that occasion is worth describing. It was in the form of a trench, about 1 yard across by 3 yards long and perhaps 4 feet (1.2 metres) deep, with plywood walls, a bench, shelves to hold cartridges, racks to hold the guns upright, and duckboards laid over a gravel floor. There was even a small charcoal brazier, for use when the weather became really cold. But the most amazing part of this comfortable dwelling was the roof. Formed of plywood, it was gently curved, to shed rain and also to be less conspicuous, and overlapped the trench by about 18 in (½ metre). The eaves were mounted on 8 in (20 cm) blocks so that we could look out from beneath the overhang without being seen from above. The really clever thing was that the roof-support blocks were mounted on small nylon wheels which ran silently in rails. When the moment came to shoot, we simply yanked on a handle, and the whole roof slid back effortlessly, like the top of a missile silo! The outside of the roof was covered in wide-mesh chicken wire, through which dead cornstalks had been woven. From the outside, the whole contraption was unrecognisable from 10 yards.

Permanent hides are rarely used in Britain nowadays, although they may have been more common several decades ago. Given the way that geese seem to favour certain fields year after year, one might think that permanent hides would have kept pace with the boom in inland goose shooting, but this is not the case. I suspect that part of the reason is the backlash against anything which smacks of excessive bags. Purpose-built pits in fields were used in the early part of this century to account for what we would now consider to be obscene bags of geese. In addition, there is a natural tendency to eschew anything which seems too civilised and comfortable, which is not really in accordance with the wildfowling origins of goose shooting. Of course, we should not accuse the North Americans of being 'soft'; during the shooting season Canada and the northern states of the USA can experience weather which is far colder than anything we ever have to cope with in this country. Protection from the elements is only secondary task for a hide in Britain, whereas in North American it may be a vital consideration.

Most of the artificial hides used in inland goose shooting are based on the techniques which have been established in pigeon decoying. The basic tools are a camouflage net and special poles which are used to support it. Years ago, the only nets available were offcuts of large military nets designed primarily to conceal vehicles and artillery from the air. Although the army used desert and snow versions, the general public normally had to make do with standard woodland scrim. As the woodland being used by the army at the time was the mixed deciduous and conifer forests of Germany, the nets were rather too dark for our winter fields, as well as being very heavy and unwieldy.

More recently, small, lightweight, purpose-built camouflage nets have become widely available in a range of colours, often with one shade on one side and another on the other. Established varieties include stubble and moorland. These are much more suitable, and it is worth seeking them out, rather than automatically settling for army netting which may have been designed for very specific conditions. The most useful unit of size for a net is a width of around 5 feet (1.5 metres) and a length of 20 feet (6 metres). With four poles arranged to hold the net in a rectangular box shape, this provides a basic hide for two people. It is possible to build a hide for three, but this is near the limit of convenience and effective concealment, and I would recommend that for more than three people, another hide should be built. At all costs, avoid the sort of enormous 'gin palace' affairs that are sometimes created by inexperienced fowlers.

The front wall of the hide should normally be a bit lower than the sides or back, although you will have to adapt each hide you build for the precise circumstances on the day. Some pigeon decoyers like to build roofs, but this is normally not a good idea for goose shooters, who may well have to take overhead shots. An exception is when you are trying to conceal yourself along the bank of an open ditch, when you could drive the poles into the top of the bank almost horizontally and drape the nets over to form a canopy. This is not ideal, however, as you then have to step out from under the net before shooting, and this may cause the geese to flare at the critical moment.

You should use locally picked grasses etc. to lend the net touches of colour from the immediate area, but do not attempt to smother the entire net – this will only result in loose material falling or blowing off, probably just as geese are coming in, as well as unnecessarily restricting your ability to see through the net. You should make sure that your tufts of vegetation stay the right way up, and pay particular attention to breaking up any unnaturally straight lines or edges, such as the top rim of the net.

Do not rely on finding suitable natural materials, such as branches, to support the net, but invest in some good home-made or shop-bought purpose-built hide poles. Some of the best have kick-plates, which enable you to get them into hard or frozen ground. I used to think that extending hide poles were an unnecessary luxury, but I have changed my mind. They provide enormous flexibility, enabling the hide to be sited on virtually any ground while maintaining a proper net height. Another advantage is that one can lower a part of the net to step in or out of the hide without disrupting the structure or treading on colleagues. Lightweight alloy poles are easier to carry than steel or iron ones, although they also tend to bend and therefore jam more easily.

The siting of a hide in relation to decoys is something we shall consider in more detail in the next chapter, but a general principle is that a hide should be sited with tactical objectives uppermost. In other words, a good hide should help to conceal you in the best *shooting* position, rather than the best *hiding* position. Of course, you will have to compromise and make the best use of existing cover, but do not try to *hide the hide* so much as use it to *hide yourself.*

Hide Discipline

Think of the scene the way a goose will see it, which is normally from a high angle. I once left a decoy set-up to look for a wounded goose, ending up on a hill 200 feet (60 metres) higher and perhaps ¼ mile (400 metres) away. Looking back down at the scene was instructive. The decoys looked astonishingly lifelike, although they were not seen at their best because of a slight dip in the ground. A sudden movement instantly caught my eye, even at that range, and I noticed something black at the edge of a gorse bush. It later turned out to be a gunslip which had slid out underneath a net. There were three hides, holding a total of five people. All three hides were fairly inconspicuous, although one was of the wrong colour (too light, as it happened, which is unusual). The size of two of the hides also made them stand out – they were noticeably larger than the gorse bushes scattered along the ruined wall. At 400 yards, with a slight breeze blowing across my front, I could easily hear one of my colleagues using a goose call.

There was more movement and my eyes were drawn again to one of the hides, although the cause was not immediately obvious. Through my binoculars, however, I could clearly see two pink faces, only partly obscured by hats, peering over the top of a net. Then they sank down again. I later discovered that they had not been standing, simply kneeling up, which shows how big a mistake it is to hoist the net too low. From a normal human viewpoint, on the ground, that hide looked high enough. But from a goose's viewpoint, it was too low and came too far out from the background (partly gorse, partly wall) to provide adequate cover.

Always look through the net, not over it. Keep the net high and tight in to the background, keep the hide small, and secure all loose kit inside it. You never really know when you are being observed by geese, so if you do have to move, do so slowly.

If you drop a goose and it runs, then you should of course retrieve it straight away. This is where a dog can be very useful, and apart from anything else the sight of a dog in the field is much less likely to scare incoming geese. If fallen geese are dead, then it is probably best to leave them where they fall, unless they have fallen belly-up, when you should turn them over. In general, however, you should leave the hide as little as possible. It is uncanny how often incoming geese seem to materialise out of thin air, invariably turning up just as someone is undoing the top of his vacuum flask, or unloading his gun to check the barrels.

Preparation and Comfort

Most goose shooters have at some time found themselves staggering about in the dark with tangled nets, hurriedly trying to build a hide while the eastern sky grows ever lighter, discovering at the last moment that there is a much better site just 10 yards away – and who forgot to bring the coffee? This sort of early morning shambles seems to be part of the tradition of goose decoying. Yet it need not be like this.

If you are confident that the wind direction will remain constant, and you know exactly where you want to place your decoys or where you expect the geese to fly, then it may make sense to build your hide the night before. This gives you time to get everything just right, making things rather less frenetic the following dawn. And if you turn out to be wrong, at least all the kit is already on site, so it will not take long to adjust it. Normally you should not put the decoys out the night before, because if there is a frost or rain, they could become shiny. But you could store them in one of the hides. One other time when you really should try to erect your hide the night before is when heavy hoar frost or snow is expected. White snow nets are available, but it is much simpler to let nature take care of all your camouflage problems for you.

For years, I shot from hides in all sorts of positions, often kneeling or sitting on the ground. It never really occurred to me to take something to sit on; somehow, it just did not seem right to get too worried about personal comfort. Now I know better. Any fool can be uncomfortable, the old army saying goes. There is also the matter of marksmanship, which is definitely impeded by a cramped position. I strongly advise you to use one of the special seats available, or to make your own. Failing this, you could buy a set of gardening knee pads, which make an enormous difference if you have to shoot from a kneeling position, without reducing your overall agility.

Clothing

An important clothing consideration is what to wear on one's head. It has to keep you warm, it should be waterproof if at all possible, and it must shield the face. The traditional choice is a broad-brimmed hat, but the simple fact is that this only conceals the face from above when the face is lowered. Although constantly peering at incoming geese is a sure way to be spotted, it is important to be able to watch them to some extent. A really good hide will do the trick in most cases, but all too often people wearing hats do not realise just how little it shields the face, and so they fail to observe proper hide discipline.

I wear an old, very thin, pale green balaclava for all my goose shooting and wildfowling these days. It completely covers my face, with holes for the eyes and mouth, and repeated washings mean that it no longer itches. I have threaded green plastic-coated garden wire through the edges of the eye holes, so that I can mould them to shape. When I am not actually shooting, I roll it up on top of my head like an ordinary woollen hat. I find I can hear through the thin knit very easily, and it keeps me warm even in the pouring rain, although it does sag a bit when it gets wet. I have tried face masks and veils, and I am sure they work for some people, but I still prefer the old balaclava.

Instead of masking your face with some form of hat you could use a face veil, or even camouflage cream. Unfortunately, the latter is quite difficult to wash off, which may give you all sorts of problems later in the day – like scaring the local populace! Many years ago I tried burnt cork, and I can assure you that it is the very devil to scrub off. If you want to be heroic, you could use good old mud – which is also very useful for camouflaging light-coloured dogs, incidentally.

Moving on to the body, there is a very wide range of effective coats and trousers available today, and I do not propose to say very much about them except to warn you not to wear anything which could disrupt your ability to swing a gun properly.

As for footwear, I tend to favour thigh waders for most decoying situations. Time after time I have found that ditches are too deep to be crossed in ordinary wellingtons, and even flooded fields can cause problems without waders. Of course, rubber is not very insulating, but I seldom get cold feet. A thin pair of cotton socks which allow my feet to move comfortably inside a pair of thick loop-stitch woollen socks is all I ever seem to need. Putting on too many socks, which cramp your feet and crush the air pockets in the wool, will invariably result in cold feet.

Nor do I suffer from cold hands, which is probably just as well, because I cannot abide wearing any of the shooting gloves available. I find the lack of feeling intolerable, and my solution is to wear sheepskin mitts which cover the backs of my hands only. It is important to cover the backs of the hands, if only because they are sometimes glaringly obvious to approaching geese.

You should also wear some form of ear protection, although I know that most of us still do not. It is true that goose shooters do not generally fire many cartridges in a session, but the real problem of noise may be caused by a muzzle blast from another gun being fired alongside you from the same hide. Unfortunately, the effects of this sort of noise may not become apparent for many years, by which time it is, of course, too late. There are some very good ear protectors on the market, which are designed to let the wearer hear sound at normal volume, only cutting out the damaging sounds. They are expensive, but they should be regarded as necessities rather than luxuries.

Equipment

The wildfowling classics are full of ways to keep cartridges dry, which makes one realise just how much easier life is today. I do not like the clutter and constraint of a cartridge belt, preferring to use my coat pockets for 12-bore cartridges and the like, while using a combination of pockets and a bag or pouch if I am using heavier ammunition. It is often necessary to reload from a cramped position when goose shooting, so the ideal would be some form of pouch or pocket which holds a quantity of ammunition at chest height, where it can be reached easily, so long as this does not interfere with the shooting shoulder.

I always try to take binoculars with me, and whenever I forget them (which is all too frequently!) I wish I had them. They make life so much more interesting, apart from anything else, although their main practical uses include spotting geese at long distance, identifying species, finding distant downed geese and general reconnaissance.

If you are going out onto the foreshore, you will need a variety of other equipment, including a compass – but make sure you know how to use it first! You will also need a powerful and reliable torch and a whistle as additional safety aids.

For carrying kit, nothing can beat a rucksack of some sort, and it is best to make sure that every piece of equipment is stowed away in this single bag, so that you are unlikely to lose anything. Decoys are best carried in a mesh bag with shoulder straps which can be folded away into a minute space when empty.

Optional kit includes vacuum flasks filled with hot drinks, food a camera or camcorder and notebook.

Dogs

It seems very unfair to put dogs at the end of a chapter on equipment, when they really deserve one of their own. Apart from anything else, a dog can add so much to the overall enjoyment of shooting. Sadly, they are not used very much in inland goose shooting, but they are almost *de rigeur* for coastal wildfowling, for very obvious reasons. I suspect that one of the reasons for the general lack of dogs inland is because of the prevalence of commercial guiding. Goose guides often have to put together parties of Guns who do not know each other, let alone the guide himself, and it must be difficult to cater for every eventuality. Unknown dogs are an unknown quantity, and many guides find it best to impose a blanket ban on dogs in the field – other than their own, of course.

But not even all guides have dogs, nor do they necessarily see a need for them. Yet I have gradually come round to the view that the sport would be better served by having more dogs in the field.

The purpose of a trained retriever is to find and retrieve wounded and otherwise irretrievable game. If a dog is well behaved and properly trained, then it will make a useful contribution to inland goose shooting, lessening the interval between a wounded bird being shot and dispatched humanely as well as retrieving the birds which inevitably fall across a river or in the midst of a bramble patch. It is quite remarkable how often geese manage to collapse in the one inaccessible spot in an otherwise open landscape. Good dogs can also be invaluable at night, where shot birds might otherwise be very difficult to find. On the other hand, a poorly behaved dog is an absolute menace in a hide, being a distraction, an irritation and very difficult to conceal.

It is a pity that the general standard of gundog training is not higher, because dogs could play a much greater role in inland goose shooting.

Chapter Seven

Tactics

S
uccessful goose shooting is a matter of getting oneself into the right place at the right time. Inevitably, a certain amount of luck comes into play, but a really competent goose shooter should be able to tilt the odds in his favour by deploying a range of tactical plans, each designed to take account of a particular situation. The deciding factors include the behaviour of geese, the terrain, conditions of weather, tide and moon, and equipment. The art is to use one's knowledge and judgement to predict the behaviour of the geese under varying conditions, and then use one's equipment and skill to get within range. Only then does marksmanship come into play.

Goose Behaviour

We have already looked at some of the more general behavioural traits of geese. Now we need to discuss how these translate into tactical considerations. At the same time, it is worth pointing out that there can never be any hard and fast rules with wild geese, any more than there can be in salmon fishing or the pursuit of any other truly wild animal in its own environment. We can observe and theorise all we like, but in reality there are no certainties, only probabilities. For every rule, there is an exception. For example, wild quarry geese are normally extremely wary, but many of us have seen them apparently displaying an incredible lack of caution. In each instance, there may have been a logical explanation, but that may not necessarily always be the case. As a species, geese behave logically, but taken as individuals in varying circumstances, they may be quite capable of bucking the system. When this ingredient is added to our imperfect knowledge of geese,

113

and a few other variables – such as weather and other changeable environmental factors – it becomes apparent that the tactics of goose shooting are more of an art than a science.

So what are the most common types of behaviour of our main quarry geese which might be useful to us? In simplified form, they are as follows.

1. *Geese generally feed by day, flighting out from their roosts on estuaries or inland waters to visit their feeding grounds at dawn, and then returning to their roosts in the evening.*
Accepting that we should not disturb the roosts, this leaves us the option of intercepting the geese on their journey between roosting and feeding grounds and vice versa, as well as arranging to meet them on their feeding grounds. This looks like a simple case of plotting a line on a map, but the reality is more complicated.

At both take-off and landing, when their airspeed is at its lowest, geese instinctively try to gain the greatest effective airflow over their wings to maintain the maximum amount of aerodynamic lift. This is why they always try to take off and land into the wind. Taking off or landing downwind would require a much greater effort, and the lack of control (like the lack of steerage in a slow-moving ship) could even cause the goose to crash and injure itself. So geese do not move in an arrow-straight line between roost and feeding grounds, but take off into the wind, then head towards their destination where, they once again head into the wind before touchdown. In general, this deflection from their chosen flightpath is much greater at take-off than landing.

This assumes, of course, that the geese have decided on their destination. In practice, they may fly around looking for a new feeding ground, or be influenced by the behaviour of preceding skeins which they have watched in the air. They will normally do a few circuits of their chosen field anyway, both to lose height and to scan for predators. Furthermore, while still *en route* they will tend to avoid strange objects, people in fields, busy roads and so on. Finally, a strong crosswind may actually push them off course, or at least cause their route between two points to 'bow' in a downwind direction.

The route may also be influenced by past experience. For example, if they have been shot at or frightened in some other way while flying over a certain point, then they will tend either to fly round that point in the near future or, if they cannot avoid it, they will increase their altitude as they fly over it. It is very common to see geese automatically rise as they approach the sea wall at morning flight.

Topography also influences the route taken. Geese tend to fly around high hills and mountains rather than embarking on a steep, energy-sapping climb,

114

and they show a preference for flying along rivers and other watercourses – although to nothing like the same extent as ducks. Topography also plays a role in adjusting a route for ease of navigation. In one particular area of Perthshire, the geese normally flight off a loch in the morning heading in one of a number of directions, depending on where they intend to feed, but at night when they flight back they invariably head for one particular area half a mile from the loch before continuing. This spot is marked on the ground by a pumphouse, and is notable for having a number of bright yellow security lights which switch on automatically as dusk falls. It seems entirely probable that the geese are using these lights as a sort of homing beacon, reorienting themselves once they are over the pumphouse for the final run home.

So plotting the likely route that geese will take is not easy. The timing of flights is simpler, but even here there are many variations. Under normal circumstances, they start to leave their roosts in the grey light of dawn, and this is itself subject to wide variation under different weather conditions. All other things being equal, they will lift later on a dark, overcast morning than on a bright, sunlit one. Geese also seem to lift later in really cold weather than they do under mild conditions. Pinkfeet seem to fly in poorer light than greylags, while my experience of whitefronts suggests that they too seem to fly earlier than greylags. Sometimes greylags wait until it is almost broad daylight before moving. Small groups of geese may start to move up to half an hour before the big battalions, and even when the latter go, it may take up to an hour before the roost is cleared. Geese which have been roosting on flashes or rivers near or actually on their feeding grounds, as occasionally happens with smallish groups, sometimes move very early, and seem to have a tendency to fly without calling. I have been caught out many times by geese behaving like this.

Having moved inland to feed, it is usual for a few small groups of geese to head back to the roost at mid-morning. On the coast, this movement is well known, and is often referred to as the goose's 'wash and brush-up' time. They usually stock up with grit, of which they seem to need a surprisingly large amount.

In midwinter, geese generally set off back to their roosts in poorer light conditions than when they left in the morning. Even greylags seem to flight back when it is virtually dark. Another contrast to the morning flight is that returning geese normally fly in just a few big skeins, rather than the trickle building to a flood which characterises the morning flight.

A major exception to the 'morning out, evening in' rhythm occurs when the moon is full or almost full and the skies are clear. Then geese will tend either to stay out on the fields or, if there is a dark period before the moonrise, return to roost as normal and then flight out again when the moon has

115

risen sufficiently. Pinkfeet are particularly likely to moonflight – they will move under as little as a quarter moon and even, in some circumstances, under particularly bright starlight. When geese have been moonflighting, their normal flighting patterns tend to become erratic, and this disruption may continue for some days after moonflighting has ceased. The morning flight, in particular, tends to become very late, or even something of a non-event.

2. *Geese generally fly out of range wherever they can.*
Geese do not like to expend energy unnecessarily, but nor do they like to fly near the ground. They may fly low over water, mudflats or sandbanks, where they can see that there are no predators or humans, but otherwise they try to take off and return to the ground fairly quickly, leaving themselves within shotgun range for relatively short periods of time. A goose taking off into a moderate breeze, without any reason for taking any particular avoiding action, will probably reach a height of 40 or 50 yards within 500 yards. If startled or suspicious they can, of course, climb much more rapidly. In most circumstances, they do not like to fly over a human at an altitude of less than about 100 yards – usually a great deal more. They often continue to climb gently even when they are well out or range, perhaps as a visual aid to navigation. When nearing their destination on morning or evening flight, they are often 200 or 300 yards high. On arrival, they can lose height without covering much ground, often by a combination of spiralling down on set wings and whiffling. In this way, they are vulnerable for the shortest possible time.

What this means is that even if we manage to position ourselves directly under flying geese, they may be far out of range. The chief exceptions are when they are intercepted either shortly after they have gone up or shortly before they come down. In practice, this means that we have to get close to their take-off point in the morning or in the evening, or we have to meet them on their feeding grounds. The problem with the first is that we must not be so close as to make the roost seem insecure, while the problem with the second and third is that we must ensure that the geese are able to feed in peace for the vast majority of the day.

There are some conditions in which geese fly much lower than usual, and these may help us. The first is wind. A really strong wind, blowing at gale force, gives the goose a considerable buffeting, just like an airliner subjected to turbulence, and may also make it difficult for the bird to make headway. Geese are capable of flying in considerable storms, but these conditions force them to use a lot of energy in keeping on course and on an even keel. During a gale, the wind speed will be lowest at ground level, becoming progressively greater with increasing altitude. This is due to the disruption of the airstream at low level by trees, hills, hedges and so on. This same 'friction' effect is the reason why gales are often more severe on coasts, which they hit after roaring unimpeded across miles of sea, than they are well inland. As a consequence, geese sometimes fly within range of gunners in a gale, especially when they have to fly directly into it, which requires the greatest effort.

Poor visibility, such as driving rain, blizzards and especially fog or mist, will also cause geese to fly within range. They will often set off on their journey much later than usual, and may be rather hesitant, sometimes setting off from the roosts in a half-hearted manner and returning after a short circuit or two. They seem to rely on visual landmarks for detailed navigation within a locality, and they will often descend through mist to keep visual contact with the ground. They also show a much greater tendency to fly along or near strong visual markers which stand out in such conditions, including pylon lines, hills and woods. They call incessantly, and the use of a goose call during these conditions, or in the dark of night or early dawn, can be extremely effective. It almost goes without saying that if you ever do find yourself in a situation where the geese are flying around confused and lost, then you should take care not to over-exploit their misfortune.

Rough, stormy weather may also aid the coastal wildfowler if the heaving seas force the roosting geese to shelter in the lee of the saltings, so possibly shortening the distance between them and the fowler and making it more likely that they will be within range if he is correctly positioned. Tides can sometimes also help by floating roosting geese in towards the merse edge over night, with much the same effect.

3. Geese like to feed in company.
Of all their behavioural characteristics, this is probably the biggest cause of the goose's downfall. It provides the basic mechanism for decoying, and decoying is arguably the most effective method of shooting geese.

Ironically, the propensity for geese to feed in flocks is almost certainly due to a need to cope with natural predators. By feeding in flocks, with a proportion of alert birds – especially at the edges – the geese have a more favourable ratio of time spent feeding in relation to watching for predators than they would if they fed singly or in family groups.

Skeins of geese leaving the roost often follow earlier skeins, and much depends upon these early pathfinders. They tend to be very wary, circling round the field where they were feeding the day before, seeming to examine every hedge and ditch to spot any hidden danger. When they do eventually land, they often choose the very middle of the field, standing still for some time with heads up and alert, before settling down and walking over to a suitable patch of ground. Logic suggests that these geese are among the

117

hungriest, which is why they have flown early, but even so they take care to make very sure that all is well before they land.

Even when other geese arrive, there is much circling round and scanning. If a bigger lot settle in another field, then the first ones – especially if they are pinkfeet, which are more gregarious than greylags – may move over to join them. As far as geese are concerned, safety really does lie in numbers. Once a feeding flock has built up, new arrivals are much happier about joining them, and will do so with just a few circuits to lose height.

4. *Geese are creatures of habit.*
Year after year, geese frequent the same fields, the same roosts and the same flightlines. If they are unduly harassed, of course, they will desert an area, as they will if the habitat undergoes a major change for the worse. They will also move to neighbouring areas if these seem more attractive for whatever reason. Pinkfeet, in particular, are highly mobile, and their surge in population over recent decades has inevitably caused them to colonise new areas. But taken overall, geese are unlikely to change their habits unless they are forced to, and it is quite remarkable how they tend to appear at the same places at the same times every year. One of the reasons for the former decline in the Greenland whitefront population is thought to be its extraordinary site fidelity, which may have caused it problems in adapting to a changing environment in some parts of its range.

Experienced goose shooters who know an area intimately will build up considerable knowledge of the geese on their territory; they will know the cycle of feeding throughout the season – which fields the geese are likely to use, and approximately when – as well as the local movements due to snow or frost, etc. This local knowledge is invaluable to the tactical considerations of goose shooting, and can never be matched by theory alone.

Having considered the tactical implications of the behaviour of geese, and with due regard for etiquette, we can now define some of the methods open to today's goose shooter using a shoulder-fired gun as follows.

Coastal flighting – intercepting the geese, chiefly at dawn, but possibly under the moon or at dusk

Inland flighting – as above, but inland

Stalking – moving within range of geese on the ground

Decoying – attracting geese within range, chiefly inland and in daytime, but also under the moon

Driving – pushing geese over waiting Guns

As a rough guide, the acceptability of these methods among the wild-fowling community decreases markedly as one moves from the top of the list downwards! Coastal flighting is the sport of the foreshore purists – and a very fine sport it is too. However, for reasons already explained, the dedicated goose shooter is unlikely to restrict himself to this form of shooting. Inland flighting also has a long and honourable history, although great care must be taken not to disturb the roosts by shooting too close to them. It is probable that relatively few geese are accounted for by inland flighting, as it is more usual nowadays to use decoys inland.

Stalking is another inland method. It seems to be fairly uncommon, probably because commercial decoying involving parties of shooters is so prevalent, but also possibly because of concern about disturbing geese on their feeding grounds. There is also a stigma attached to shooting 'sitting' targets with a shotgun (although in practice many stalks entail shooting at geese as they take wing). BB thoroughly approved of stalking, considering it to be a real challenge to get within range of a goose; he thought it was one of the most exciting forms of goose shooting. Even Noel Sedgewick, writing in *The New Wildfowler*, seems to have accepted stalking, while roundly condemning decoying. Bill Powell, another anti-decoyer, was also a great exponent of stalking.

Decoying could conceivably take place on the foreshore, particularly the saltings, but many clubs do not allow it. As it is, the vast majority of decoying takes place inland. Decoying is condemned by a minority of shooters, but in general it is accepted as a valid tactic *provided that the etiquette is not breached*.

Driving has a very bad name in some areas, although it cannot be intrinsically wrong. It can be combined with decoying and even stalking in some circumstances. Once again, it all depends on observing the etiquette.

We shall consider each method in turn.

Coastal Flighting

This is wildfowling proper, where the shooter has to make the most of any opportunity. Consequently, few 'saltwater gunners' restrict themselves to geese. The etiquette of the foreshore demands that one pass up the chance of a shot at a passing mallard at dawn if geese are expected, but the fact is that relatively few geese are shot on the foreshore nowadays, for reasons that we have already discussed.

The basic tactic for a morning flight on the coast is to try to ascertain where the geese are roosting (it should normally be possible to hear them, even if they are up to half a mile away) and place oneself where, given the behavioural factors discussed above, they might be intercepted when they rise.

The best chance of shooting a goose on the foreshore is likely to be during very rough weather; the ideal conditions are a combination of poor visibility, a strong headwind keeping the geese low at morning flight, and deep snow inland which forces the geese to spend more time in the vicinity of the saltings, which may stay green and inviting due to being washed by successive tides. Such a combination does not happen very often, however. I think it must be significant that most of the geese I have seen shot on the foreshore were either single birds or in small groups, and were flying around at 'wash and brush-up' time in mid-morning or mid-afternoon, when most fowlers had left the area. The big skeins seen during the main flight times at dawn and dusk seem to be better at looking after themselves and much less likely to fly within range of the saltings.

There is a school of thought which says that the best place to conceal oneself is not out on the mudflats or the sands, or even the saltings, where one really has to stay put once the flight has begun, but behind the sea wall, where one might be able to run under the passing skeins once the first has indicated the flightline. I have used this technique to good effect under the moon, but at more popular flight times there is the risk of ending up several hundred yards inland of other fowlers out on the tideline, with the result that even if one does manage to get under the geese they will be too high by the time they are overhead. In addition, the geese in many areas have developed an habitual suspicion of the sea wall and habitually cross it several gunshots high.

The amount of disturbance on the foreshore and the area immediately inland is a major factor affecting the height at which the geese fly. Most shots at geese on the foreshore are necessarily taken at something approaching maximum range, but there are exceptions. In fact, the closest I have ever come to naturally flighting quarry geese was on the foreshore. I was walking on the saltings in an area to the north of Wigtown Bay, in south-west Scotland, when I heard geese on the grass fields just inland of the sea wall, which in that area is a fairly inconspicuous embankment 6 feet (2 metres) high with gently sloping sides covered in grass. The sun had just set. I crawled up to the top of the embankment and peered through a ragged clump of thistles. There were about 200 pinkfeet feeding not a hundred yards away. The light wind was at my back, and the geese were feeding into it, making the weird guzzling, buzzing noise that indicates contentment.

A sudden increase in gabbling raised the hairs on the back of my neck; the geese bunched, there was a thunder of wings and they were off. I flattened myself into the rough grass on the reverse slope. They came over me in three successive waves, not 3 yards above me as I lay on my back. I am sure I could feel the downdraft of their huge wings on my upturned face, and the noise of their calling seemed to make my ears ring. As they climbed into the glowing western sky, silhouetted for a moment before wheeling towards the distant Baldoon Sands, they looked like Lancaster bombers leaving an East Anglian airfield to raid Germany. I felt as though I had been at the end of the runway.

I should explain that it was a Sunday and, this being Scotland, I was armed with nothing more lethal than a walking stick. The bizarre thing is that I could have jumped up and hit them with it! I am not at all sure that I would have tried it even if it had not been the Sabbath; and even if I had, nobody would have believed me anyway!

I suppose the real lesson is that if one spends enough time on the foreshore, and is utterly dedicated, then one may strike lucky. But do not count on it.

Inland Flighting

I am convinced that much of the inland flighting described in the classic works of wildfowling would be well outside the accepted etiquette of today, largely because it often seemed to involve shooting on roosts. And even where it did not, it often meant waiting for the geese on or very near their feeding grounds, so the foreshore purist's grudging acceptance of inland flighting while refusing to countenance decoying seems rather misplaced.

If we accept that roosts must never be disturbed and that geese must be allowed to feed without undue harassment on the fields, then we are left with few opportunities for inland flighting. In contrast to the situation with coastal flighting, where the morning flight generally offers the best chance, the evening flight is probably best for an inland flight.

The problem with the morning flight inland is that it invariably involves waiting for the geese near their feeding grounds, unless they can be flighted coming off an inland water in the morning, which we shall look at later. Trying to intercept geese near their feeding grounds risks disturbing their feeding every bit as much as decoying – so why not decoy in the first place? Given that geese generally fly out of range until they reach their destination, one is unlikely to find them flying low enough anywhere along the route.

There are exceptions, of course. I have in mind one particular part of Scotland where the geese sometimes choose to fly through a high pass in the hills to reach certain fields in the strath beyond. When the wind is strong enough, and blowing from just the right quarter, the shape of the land seems to funnel the wind in such a way that the geese seem to struggle to fly higher than about 30 yards as they top the pass. In the right conditions, the shooting is tremendous, with the added bonus of a truly magnificent view. One goose bagged here at morning flight really does seem to be worth two gained in less spectacular surroundings. But this place probably only comes into its own for less than a week in total each season.

Shooting geese as they flight off an inland roost in the morning can be good sport, but there is always the danger of disturbing the roost. Unlike the foreshore, where the distances are vast and the noise of gunfire is easily soaked up by the wide open spaces and the rumble of surf and wind, the area around inland roosts may be wooded, or the land may be formed so that shots fired from the best positions echo and reverberate, causing alarm among the birds yet to depart. The best compromise may be to choose a point where the Guns can line out along a hedge or ditch on the reverse side of a slope, so that the sound is muffled and its direction is disguised.

The evening flight inland was traditionally held at the roost itself, but of course this is no longer regarded as acceptable by the vast majority of fowlers. If you can find a spot which is far enough from the roost but where the geese fly within range, then that is fine – but such places are rare. While most geese return to their roost at a great height, however, some small parties seem to fly much lower – especially if they come in when the light has gone.

I recall one evening flight in Angus when we strung out along a stone wall which ran across a gap between two large woods. We were about ½ mile (800 metres) from the roost, which was a large loch. A few big skeins of pinkfeet came in, 200 yards high, but nothing came within range as the darkness gathered. We were about to pack up, when the Gun on my left shouted. Three geese loomed straight at me over the brow of the hill, flying at head height like giant driven partridge. He fired and hit one, and the shot caused the other two to tower as they went between us. This gave me a chance, and I got a right-and-left – snap shooting with an eight-bore! Perhaps these geese had been feeding by themselves nearby, but it is equally likely that they were flying so low because it was too dark to see the ground from much further up and they were simply heading for the gap between the two woods.

Perhaps the most effective form of inland flighting involves intercepting geese as they leave their feeding grounds and head back to their roost. This was the situation in the evening flight I described at the beginning of Chapter 5. The trick here is to get close enough to the geese so that they are still within range when they come over, but without spooking them or giving them any cause to avoid the hiding place. Once again, stone walls are a boon, as they may allow you to run or adjust your position once the geese are up and you can see which way they are headed. In calm conditions it may be very difficult to work out their initial bearing on take-off, although the trade-off is that their rate of climb will be lower. If you have a party of Guns, you may be able to work out a sophisticated plan whereby one Gun's firing will turn the geese across the front of the line. I have also seen people leave cars, dogs and other people in prominent positions so as to divert geese away from a particular route.

It is seldom possible to get more than a couple of shots during this sort of a flight, as the geese tend to come over in one or two big groups. A particular concern is picking up, as the increasing darkness could conceivably make it difficult to spot or mark a wounded bird. Another important consideration is the birds' feeding requirements; especially in midwinter, when the days are short, it is generally regarded as a breech of etiquette to flush the birds. Instead, you should normally allow them to jump of their own accord.

Stalking

I can vouch for the fact that stalking is, at its best, very arduous and exciting – and a successful outcome is far from guaranteed! Stalking is not much practised nowadays, and one of the concerns is that it usually entails shooting geese on their feeding grounds. In order to fall in line with current etiquette, you should probably restrict your stalking activities to the first couple of hours after dawn, and preferably only stalk relatively small parties of geese. The reason for stalking first thing in the morning rather than in the afternoon is that in the early morning geese customarily fly around a good deal anyway, whereas by late afternoon they may be fully settled. If they are pushed off then, their feeding may be abruptly curtailed for the rest of the day and they may not be able to catch up. In addition, they will probably have to search out an entirely new feeding area the next morning. As a goose may have to spend virtually every daylight hour feeding in midwinter, this sort of disruption should be avoided.

The object of stalking is to get within range of geese on the ground. This means using cover, which is where the problems begin. For a start, geese seldom feed within range of cover. (I have occasionally found their droppings right up to ditches and fences – sometimes in the ditch itself – but this is rare, and seems to be restricted to instances where the geese have been exceptionally well settled in a field, having used it for a long time.) The next problem is that most goose country is flat, bare and totally devoid of cover of any sort. Much of Bill Powell's stalking involved barnacle geese, which are merse feeders. While it may look flat, the merse is in fact intersected by a multitude of creeks and gullies, and these provide excellent cover.

Old books on wildfowling used to refer to all sorts of devious devices for

creeping up on geese. Sometimes real animals were used as a shield, and sometimes an animal was constructed out of canvas and other materials, hence the term 'stalking horse'. Artificial animals were still being widely used in the early twentieth century. Stanley Duncan and Guy Thorne's authoritative work, *The Complete Wildfowler*, first published in 1911, contains details of the proper deployment of artificial stalking animals. Indeed, the authors state casually: 'An artificial sheep in which the gunner can ensconce himself is a very useful and as a rule successful tool of the wildfowler'!

Another problem is that feeding geese move, sometimes quite rapidly, and by the time the stalker has crept up on them in one place, they could have eaten their way halfway across the field. Skilled stalkers will take account of a flock's likelihood of moving, and factor it into their calculations.

Lastly, there is the problem of safety. Crawling around in the mud and crouching down as you wade carefully along ditches may be excellent exercise, but it is hardly conducive to the safe handling of a weapon. At the very least, mud can easily plug the muzzle of the gun. I believe that BB used to insert a large cork in the barrel of 'Belching Bess', his single eight-bore, when embarking upon a stalk, but I would not recommend this – you might forget the cork! Deerstalkers often cover the muzzle of their rifle with a bit of tape which they simply shoot through, but a rifle barrel is entirely different from a fragile shotgun tube, and I certainly do not recommend obstructing a shotgun barrel in any way whatsoever.

Keeping a gun loaded during the actual stalk, as some people do, provides almost endless permutations of possible disaster. Bill Powell records how he was lucky to escape death once when a man crawling along right behind him accidentally discharged his gun, missing Powell by inches. After that, he never allowed anybody other than the front man to carry a loaded gun. I would go further, and strongly advise that all guns be unloaded and, moreover, in their slips. This will allow the gun to be slid along the ground and passed through hedges without any danger of foreign bodies becoming lodged in the barrels, or twigs snatching at the triggers. Then, at the optimum point, it can be taken out and loaded. This manoeuvre may be rather awkward, but then the whole stalk is likely to be awkward!

Local knowledge and a pair of good quality binoculars are invaluable in planning a stalk. An innocent-looking ditch, burbling along sweetly with what seems to be a few inches of clear running water, may turn out to be thigh deep in evil-smelling ooze, having been dug out the winter before and subsequently choked with decaying vegetation. The important thing is to work out what the terrain looks like from a feeding goose's viewpoint. The most tactically useful cover is seldom the most obvious. Dead ground, for instance, formed by the humps and gentle undulations of the land, is difficult to spot from a distance. The dead grass stems supported by the wire at the foot of a fence may give more than enough cover, as might the most scrawny of hedges – or even the tufts of grass and thistles in a corner of rough pasture. Often, the furrow around the edge of a ploughed field is deep enough to hide a man lying flat, although progress along one of these will be very slow and undignified!

Above all, do not rush. Plan your route carefully, and remember the old army adage that time spent on reconnaissance is seldom wasted. In particular, you should carefully note places at which you may be able to observe the geese, and select markers to show you how close you are to them and their precise position.

Bill Powell reckoned that the ideal number of people for a stalk was one! Furthermore, he gave the average odds of this single person getting within range as being two to one, and widened them proportionately for each additional Gun. Considering safety as well, stalking parties should generally be kept to no more than two people. Any others who wish to participate (as opposed to observing from a distance) should be positioned to intercept the geese as and when the stalkers manage to fire or flush them.

Once you have set off on the stalk, take it steadily and calmly. Resist the temptation to keep poking your head above cover to look at the geese, and if you do need to do so, remember the principles of camouflage and concealment. Do not worry too much about noise. Geese do not seem too concerned about noise – even the human voice – although an unusual or incongruous noise may draw their attention to suspicious movement.

A real difficulty is estimating when you are within range. For some reason, geese look very much closer on the ground than they do in the air – especially if they are well lit by bright sunlight against a dark background, such as plough or grass. You should of course resist the temptation to take too long a shot, even if that is all that is available to you after a particularly knee-crunching, backaching, hand-scratching ordeal lasting an hour!

Assuming that all has gone as planned, how should you take the shot? Once again, matters are simplified if there are no more than two of you. You can choose your birds, and shoot on a count. Resist the temptation to 'brown' into the flock, of course, and in my experience, trying for a 'cannon' usually results in neither bird being cleanly killed. Instead, choose a single bird, with another in mind for your other shot. Whether to shoot them sitting or flying is a difficult decision. Do not worry about sporting convention – the sport has been in getting in range in the first place. What we really want at this stage is a clean kill, with minimal risk of wounding. If your goose is facing you, with its chest exposed, I would advise you to shoot it sitting. Your next shot will almost invariably be at a flying goose.

But if your goose is in any other position, then some of the vital areas will be shielded, not least by the folded wings. In this case I would flush the birds by showing myself, and shoot while they have spread wings.

It is a curious fact that many otherwise excellent shotgunners are no good at hitting static targets. Given that your heart will be thumping, and your breathing laboured with the effort of the stalk and the excitement, do not think for a moment that it is all over when you get the chance of a shot! A lot can still go wrong, all of which only adds to the attraction of stalking as a thoroughly sporting tactic for shooting geese, even if it can only be used occasionally

Decoying

Without a shadow of doubt, decoying is *the* tactic for goose shooting. We have already aired the chief ethical concerns, so it almost goes without saying that the code of etiquette should be strictly followed. With that clearly understood, what we shall examine now is the mechanism of decoying.

In simple terms, the purpose of the decoys is to attract geese within range. This does not necessarily imply that the geese actually have to land, or even intend to land, with the decoys – they are simply required to be attracted within range. I make this distinction because one sometimes hears people complaining that the geese would not decoy, when in fact the decoys performed as well as could be expected, and the Guns did not take their chances because they were waiting for the geese to behave like feral pigeons. Admittedly, deciding when to shoot can be difficult, as we will discuss later. But we should bear in mind the basic task of a decoy, which it can accomplish in a number of ways.

Decoys come in many shapes and sizes, and I think it is important to choose the right ones. There is a common view that many of the more expensive and realistic decoys are designed more to attract the hunter than the hunted. Certainly, geese have been successfully decoyed with all manner of objects, including paper plates in certain circumstances, as we shall see later. But, all other things being equal, I would always choose to use the most realistic decoys I could find. Exactly how much of a difference it makes I am not sure, but what I am sure of is that it *does* make a difference. Many professional guides will tell you that geese become distinctly decoy shy by the end of the season, and it stands to reason that they will be particularly wary of any tell-tale signs that give the game away. The point was once made by Alan Myers when I complimented him on his excellent decoys. 'If there were any better ones on the market, I'd have bought them already,' he said.

Some years ago the Americans carried out a series of experiments to establish how ducks responded to a variety of decoys of varying degrees of realism. These experiments showed that the ducks were statistically much more likely to pitch into or pass close by the more realistic decoys than the less realistic ones. On that basis, there seems to be little point in compromising, but in reality there are many other factors to take into account, including weight (which may influence the number of decoys you can set out), species, durability, ability to cope with wind, rain or frost, ease of setting out, potential for modification and, of course, cost.

All our quarry grey geese will come in to grey goose decoys, regardless of the actual species depicted. This may seem to contradict my faith in realism, but what really matters is the realism of the whole decoy picture. I am sure that greylags would prefer to pitch among other greylags, and whitefronts among others of their own species. Indeed, I have often watched these two species feeding on the same field, each group keeping pretty well to itself, without much intermingling. So no doubt greylags would be best attracted to greylag decoys, with prominent orange bills, for instance, but they will come to any realistic decoy pattern using grey goose decoys. As for Canadas, they will pitch in to grey goose decoys, although no doubt Canada decoys would do even better. I am not sure whether grey geese will pitch in to Canada decoys, but I suspect they might.

The art of decoying is to present the most lifelike and realistic picture possible in a particular situation – the right number of decoys, set out in a convincing pattern, in a likely spot, backed up by skilled calling. To some extent, you will have to compromise on all these aspects, but as long as the overall picture looks right, without any glaring errors, your decoy layout should work. One of the most controllable of all these variables is the realism of your decoys, which is why it makes sense to buy the very best – by which I mean the most lifelike and convenient.

Types of Decoy

Dead geese are, in one sense, the most realistic decoys of all, and I know many professional goose guides who would always rather use dead birds than artificial decoys. One of the key advantages is that they never shine in the sun, unlike many plastic decoys, especially when covered with melting frost or rain. Of course, there are all sorts of practical problems with using dead birds – not least being the fact that one needs to shoot some in the first place! Moreover, propped-up dead geese do not necessarily look lifelike. If you do intend to use dead birds, you must set them up with the white tail coverts showing clearly – these are an important recognition point for grey geese. You can also prop some of the heads up with either a sharp stick or a thin piece of stiff wire, with the sharpened point pushed up into the bird's skull.

The Canada is now a serious pest in some areas, having undergone something of a population explosion since the 1960s. (Joe Blossom/NHPA)

Barnacle geese often form dense flocks. Note how conspicuously piebald they appear — much more so than Canadas. (Laurie Campbell/NHPA)

Bean geese often look browner than other grey geese. Note the bill, which is notably different to that of the pinkfoot, and the orange legs. (Derek Karp/NHPA)

The vital area of a goose is surprisingly small, as demonstrated on this greylag. The white lines are at intervals of one foot.

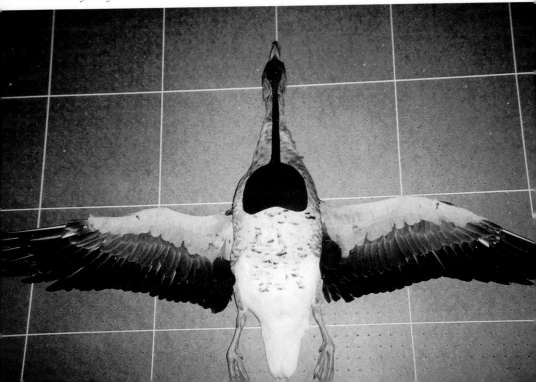

RIGHT: *Douglas McDougall wrote one of the classics of modern goose shooting, entitled* Goose Fever. *This portrait of him was painted by D. J. Watkins-Pitchford (BB). (Keith McDougall)*

BELOW: *Most fowlers consider that two geese an acceptable bag for a flight. Note the brown heads and necks of these two pinkfeet.*

RIGHT: *Alan Myers properly camouflaged in a hide. The gun is a rare Dickson double 8-bore.*

BELOW: *This net hide was built in the pre-dawn darkness against the sparse cover of a wire fence and was successful in concealing two gunners, a labrador and their assorted kit. The sloping sides help it to blend in. Ideally, the dead thistles woven into the background fence should be extended, and the bare pole at the bottom left should be covered.* (Simon Purefoy)

Pinkfoot propped up next to a shell decoy. Dead birds do not necessarily look lifelike. (Mike Swan)

These very realistic flexible full-body decoys are American, hence they are coloured as whitefronts.

Alternatively, you could place the beak through the loop in the top of a decoy peg.

The most realistic artificial decoys are the full-bodied versions, normally made of moulded plastic. These are manufactured abroad, like most of our goose decoys, and are generally coloured up as bean geese if they come from Europe, or whitefronts if they are American. There is probably not much to be gained adapting them for greylags or pinkfeet, unless you tend overwhelmingly to encounter one rather than the other of these species.

Some full-body decoys are soft and flexible, being designed to pack up into a small space. This enables you to carry a great many, but on the other hand they can be a bit of a nuisance to assemble, requiring a certain amount of fiddling about with internal supports and jointed poles. This can make things rather hectic in the cold and pre-dawn darkness. The rigid decoys, on the other hand, take up a lot of space, and if you want to use big layouts you may need to transport them in a trailer.

Various types of shell decoy have become very popular, and some of these are very well coloured and shaped. The great advantage of the shell design is that they are light and stackable, so a large number can be carried. They are also very easy to lay out, and most people do not even bother to peg them unless it is windy. There are also some very light versions which are mounted on pegs in such a way that they rock gently in the breeze.

Silhouette decoys range from simple, home-made plywood cut-outs, sometimes only painted a single dark grey colour, to more elaborate manufactured versions – sometimes featuring high-resolution photographs of real geese. Silhouettes can work well in conditions of poor visibility such as moonlight, but the problem with using them in more conventional situations is that they effectively disappear as the birds fly over them. They may be convenient, but they are not particularly realistic.

There are three situations in which relatively unrealistic, oversimplified decoys will often work: in conditions of poor visibility; when a vast number of decoys is used to create an overwhelming picture; and when dealing with young or inexperienced geese, typically in remote areas where shooting is uncommon. Indians in subarctic Canada decoy snow geese with shaped mounds of mud or snow, sometimes with goose wings folded alongside. In this country pinkfeet have been successfully decoyed under the moon by white paper plates, which presumably resemble the tail coverts of feeding birds. However, this type of simplistic decoy (which is normally supported by calling) is generally used in an area which the geese are already using with confidence. In addition, the poor light aids the deception. I very much doubt whether the same type of decoy would work with the same geese in daylight.

American hunters sometimes use huge numbers of decoys, especially for snow geese, which generally fly in flocks of several hundred. They may put down vast patterns comprising a mix of decoys, with the core made up of wind-supported plastic bags on sticks, white rags, or even empty plastic bottles. Setting out these patterns, which may number up to 1,000 decoys, may take several hours – much longer than the flighting, in fact.

Finally, various flapping, moving or 'flying' decoys are sometimes used, often in the form of a very thin, flat, plastic goose shape with wings outstretched which is mounted several feet above the ground on a springy pole, so that its wings rock and wag in the wind and supposedly give the impression of a goose about to land. Some Americans even use goose-shaped kites to support snow goose patterns!

I am sure that a certain amount of movement is very useful in a decoy pattern, adding the final touch of realism as well as attracting attention to the decoys in the first place. Pigeon decoyers have long used the trick of throwing a dead bird out of the hide to catch the attention of distant birds. Various people have tried to develop goose 'flapper' decoys, or even cradles to use dead geese, but I am not aware of any that are commercially available. I suspect that most people do not bother because they already achieve satisfactory results with conventional decoys.

Sizes of Decoy

Most artificial decoys are slightly oversize. There are, of course, so-called magnum decoys, which are considerably larger than life-size, and even truly giant super-magnum shell decoys, which are about 6 feet (2 metres) long with heads which stand 4 feet (1.2 metres) off the ground! But the most thoroughly over-the-top giant decoys are the enormous decoy/blinds made by some American firms where the shooter crouches inside a gigantic plastic goose. At the right moment, he flings open a hatch and blazes away!

I have shot over super-magnum decoys and can vouch for the fact that they work well. Inevitably, fewer big decoys are used in a pattern than would be the case with standard ones, if only because of the problems of transporting and carrying them. Yet whether six super-magnums are more effective than 12 magnums or 24 standard decoys is debatable. On balance, I think I would choose the greater number of smaller decoys, which would lend themselves better to building up a realistic picture.

The principle of using oversize decoys is well established, although nobody seems entirely sure why it works. Some have suggested that larger birds look well fed, but I am convinced that birds, like humans, find it very difficult to judge size at a distance and without obvious points of reference. I have watched geese land among super-magnum decoys. After a moment on the ground, it seems to dawn on them that all is not as it should be, and they invariably depart, although without undue haste. In this, their reaction seems little different from that of birds landing among standard decoys.

Only in America! This gigantic 'Trojan goose' is manufactured by Neumann & Bennetts of Klamath, Oregon. (Photo – Neumann & Bennetts).

It seems to me to be most likely that the pulling power of giant decoys is due to their sheer visibility. The geese can see them from a great distance, and are much less likely to fly past without at least investigating.

Patterns

Decoyers of BB's generation seem to have used small numbers of decoys, often no more than half a dozen. This may have been because they often used stuffed birds, which led to all sorts of practical problems, or perhaps the tactic was simply less developed than it is today. The important thing is to use enough decoys to create a natural-looking picture for the geese, with due regard for practical matters like the ease of transporting your equipment. As a rule, greylags, whitefronts and Canadas can be attracted with relatively small decoy patterns, while the more gregarious pinkfeet are less likely to be impressed by a small spread. Nonetheless, single birds and small skeins may come in to small patterns, and if the geese are really intent on coming in to a field they will probably come whether there are decoys out or not.

Generally, the more decoys there are, the greater their pulling power. I have successfully shot greylags over six decoys, but most professional goose guides that I know seem to use 30 or 40, and I have shot with at least one who would not dream of using less than 50, and often uses considerably more.

131

It seems that different types of decoy can be mixed, as long as they are roughly similar in size. A common practice is to use a few full-bodied decoys around the fringes of a pattern, with the main bulk being made up of the lighter and more convenient shell-type ones. Mixing decoys of greatly varying sizes, however, is not recommended.

On a day with a light to moderate breeze, geese tend to land and feed about 5 or 6 feet (1.5–2 metres) apart, but on a really windy day they seem to allow themselves up to twice as much room for manoeuvre. The spacing of decoys should take this into account. There is always a temptation to space decoys out very widely as a matter of course, if only to cover more ground in the hope of making the pattern look more impressive. You can certainly use wider spacing with oversize decoys, but remember that the overall picture must look as natural as possible; wild geese seldom feed more than about 8 feet (2.4 metres) apart.

Deciding on the right mix of feeding and alert decoys provides an interesting conundrum. Most people seem to gravitate more readily towards alert decoys, and I have seen many patterns where the upright decoys outnumber the feeding versions. But more conventional patterns have about 30 per cent alert to 70 per cent feeders. We have to remember that we are not using decoys to attract people, but geese, and the fact is that geese are much less impressed by head-up decoys than we are! Experiments have proved that they are more readily attracted to flocks which appear to be settled than ones which appear to be alert. Researchers believe that this allows them to keep abreast of the best feeding opportunities, and skeins have been seen to bypass feeding flocks with large numbers of alert geese and instead pitch in among flocks where virtually every goose had its head down.

In view of this, it may be better to try a smaller proportion of head-up decoys – perhaps no more than 15 per cent. Alan Myers often uses an interesting variation on this theme, laying out a big pattern of mainly head-down feeders, with a much smaller family group of head-up decoys off to one side, looking as if they have just landed and are in the process of walking in to join the others.

Although geese invariably land into the wind, they tend to walk around and feed in all directions when they are on the ground, although the general trend will be to face more into the wind than otherwise. Only on really windy days, when their feathers could be ruffled and blown out of order, do all feeding geese face into the wind all the time. This needs to be taken into account when laying out decoys.

Pigeon shooters have developed all sorts of fancy patterns, shaped like Vs, Ts, Ls, crosses, etc., all of which are designed to funnel the landing birds into a particular 'killing zone' which is at the optimum point for the concealed shooter. All I can say is that I have tried virtually all of these patterns with geese, but they do not seem to take much notice of my careful arrangements. Many goose shooters swear by a crescent-shaped pattern, with the point heading into the wind and the killing ground immediately behind the thickest part of the pattern, between the two arms. I often use this pattern myself, but in truth I am not sure that it does much more than give me confidence – which is a valid factor in its own right!

Reconnaissance

Dawn is the best time to scan the skies for geese heading out to feed, and the direction of the successive skeins should lead you to their chosen feeding areas.

It is possible to decoy geese off a flightline, but the more efficient method is to find out where they are feeding and then plan to ambush them there at dawn flight. Geese normally settle onto a feeding area and then stay there until the food supply dwindles, unless they are disturbed in the meantime. Farmers can often put them off, either deliberately or in the course of going about their everyday business on the land. Unless the geese are harassed, they do not seem to make a distinction between inadvertent and deliberate disturbance – after all, how could they? – so the problem is that geese feeding quietly on a field at midday might be put off and end up somewhere completely different an hour later. The chances are that the next morning they will return to where they were feeding most recently, rather than the field where they spent most of the day. This means that, unless you know for certain that they will not be disturbed during the day, you should carry out a further reconnaissance in the late afternoon to be reasonably sure of connecting with the geese the next morning.

Geese will tend to come in most readily to decoys placed on land which they have used well for several days or even weeks without much disturbance, but there is always the danger that the morning you arrive is when they decide to move on to fresh ground. Really hungry geese feed at an astonishing rate, pecking as much as 80 times a minute. A lot of the food they eat passes straight through them, especially if it is grass rather than grain, and they defecate every three or four minutes, so you should not necessarily assume that hundreds of droppings on a field indicates hundreds of geese. Grain is more nutritious than grass, but it is seldom available to the birds for any length of time. Big, hungry flocks of geese can clean up a stubble field in two or three days and never return, whereas smaller flocks might stay on a small grass field for several weeks, and return at intervals throughout the season. Geese feeding on grain seem to become thirsty, and are especially fond of fields with flashes of fresh water.

How many geese make up a decent flight? It depends partly on the number of Guns, and also on the species of goose. Given a party of four

Guns and a self-imposed bag limit of, say, eight birds, a grazing flock of as few as 50 greylags arriving in the morning in four or five skeins would give everybody a chance. With pinkfeet, on the other hand, there might not be the same chance unless there were 200 or 300 birds on the field the day before.

One additional consideration concerns livestock. I have seen geese in the Spey Valley feeding right up to sheep, but cattle seem to disconcert them. They can also severely disconcert shooters! Some of my most unpleasant moments have been spent trying to keep my composure while an apparently carnivorous Friesian bull bellowed and blew froth into my face as I cowered behind a few strands of barbed wire. If you have cattle in the field, they will invariably trample your decoys and crowd around your hide, so avoid such places.

Deployment

The best deployment is one which manages to place the decoys on a thoroughly 'goosey' patch of ground within easy range of a hide site which is inconspicuous. In typical goose country, ditches, fencelines, areas of rough pasture and stone walls tend to fit the bill for a hide site. Geese almost always aim to land on the far side of decoys, i.e. the side away from any cover, so you should normally place your pattern so that the nearest decoys are about 25 yards away from your own position, perhaps with an isolated one at 35 yards to act as a range marker. If you place them much closer to cover than this, it looks unnatural and you also run the risk of attracting attention to your own position. Moreover, you may cause the birds to flare as you move to shoot. Any further away, however, and decoying birds may be out of range. A wind blowing alongside linear cover, like a hedge, may make things easier, although placing any more than a couple of Guns in the prime spot may then become problematical.

The classic shots at decoying geese are at birds which, being committed to landing, are slowing up and dropping on fixed cupped wings, with their legs down and ready. But you should not forget that they are also vulnerable any time they are within range – circling round the decoys, on approach, and on departure. This means that you can deploy your decoys and Guns in endless permutations to suit particular circumstances. You could, for instance, place two Guns in a single small hide near the pattern's expected killing zone, and place two more along a hedge 100 yards away to intercept the geese as they depart after they have been shot at over the decoys.

In some areas it may be impossible to hide the Guns near enough to where the geese land. In these situations you could try setting the decoys out in a likely spot, with the Guns well hidden some distance away on the

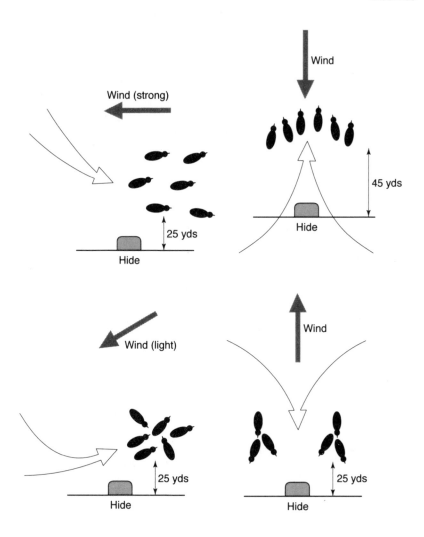

estimated line of departure. One member of the party could then put the geese up from a direction opposite the Guns once the birds have landed. This, of course, is driving, and not everyone would accept it as a sporting proposition.

Another long-distance tactic involves concealing the Guns some distance downwind of the decoys, and intercepting the geese as they fly over them *en route* to the decoys. The chief risk here is that geese often tend to swirl into a decoy pattern from one side, rather than approaching directly into the wind from some distance.

Where the circumstances demand that the decoys be placed out of range downwind of the Guns, you could try using the alarm call or giving a loud whistle just as the geese come in to settle on the decoys. With luck, this will cause them to lift into the wind and come straight over you.

Lying snow provides an interesting point of difference between pigeon decoying and goose decoying. Whereas pigeons are often difficult to attract to a pattern laid out on snow, geese are the very opposite. I am indebted to Alan Myers for a particularly effective tactic for decoying geese on snow, which should be used with restraint and discretion. By placing camouflage nets on the ground, and putting decoys on top of the nets, you can give the impression of an oasis of greenery in a desert of snow. This sometimes seems to draw the geese like wasps to a jam jar. A variation on the same theme, if you do not have enough netting, is to clear or scuff up the snow with your boots or a bushy branch; this creates much the same effect.

Decoying under the moon is subject to the same principles as normal decoying, with moonrise taking the place of dawn. I have said you may be able to use much simpler decoys, and you will also be able to hide in any convenient patch of shadow. Moonflighting is very exciting when it works well (which is rather less frequently than one might think). Ideally, a thin fleece of cloud should cover the sky in order to silhouette the birds. Retrieving shot birds can be a problem at night, so this is one of those occasions when a trained dog is essential.

Calling

I wish I were better at calling geese. Moreover, I wish some of the other people I shoot with were a lot better than they are! For some strange reason criticising somebody's ability to use a goose call is invariably taken as an insult, on a par with criticism of their children or (much worse) their dog!

There is no doubt that calling can be very effective, especially with small groups of geese in conditions of poor visibility; it can be absolutely deadly in fog. But there is also little doubt that many of us overdo it to the point where it becomes counter-productive. Geese on their roost shortly before flight time make a considerable din, which can usually be heard from a great distance. This may give some people the idea that calling is always effective. But a decoy picture is not intended to imitate roosting geese, but a contentedly feeding flock. If you crawl close and listen to geese on the ground, you will find that although they can make quite a babble at times, the overwhelming background noise made by a settled feeding flock is an extraordinary sort of soft, buzzing hum – a rather nasal sound, which seems to result from the birds having their heads down and their beaks full of food. Interspersed with this are cackles and yaps as individual geese tease each other and squabble. When new, incoming geese arrive in the air near a feeding flock, there tends to be an interchange of conventional contact calls, but this is generally fairly brief.

The notable thing about expert callers is that they know when to stop, quite unlike novices, who tend to call too much. The first objective of calling is to attract attention to the decoy pattern. There is little point in calling very large skeins, or those that are very high and obviously headed for a point miles away. Small groups of geese, and those that are flying around in a rather aimless fashion, are a much better bet. If you can solicit an answering call from a skein, then you are definitely exerting some influence.

Having attracted the attention of flying geese, your next objective is to use your call to add realism to your decoy picture. This means providing a background of feeding buzz, with a few contact calls. Do not worry that the geese will not be able to hear you – the average goose call carries much further than one might think. You should switch to the feeding buzz as the geese come closer. If they set their wings, many people say that you should stop calling altogether. This may be good advice for a novice, who is likely to make a mistake, like moving, just as the geese are bearing down with their eyes scanning the vicinity of the pattern. Yet geese often fly right over a pattern at some height before whiffling or planing down in a spiral, and it may seem unnatural to them if the feeding buzz seems to stop abruptly. If you can continue calling, and there seems to be a need for it, then do so. But if in any doubt, stop.

Suspicious geese often seem to make a series of short, sharp calls, a bit like a loud ticking, which I can only describe as a sequence of 'ka, ka, ka', with the rest of the skein usually keeping silent. This noise normally means that the geese have seen something they do not like, and they are unlikely to come in. When they have departed, you should check to see what the problem might be – whether a decoy has rolled over, or a dead bird has been left lying on its back, or there has been a problem with an unruly dog.

The alarm call of grey geese is a sharp, loud, urgent and relatively high-pitched 'kack, kack, kack' call. They will give this if they see a human and it has an immediate effect on all the geese in the flock.

There are only two really effective ways of learning how to call. The best is to ask an expert to teach you, but failing this, there are a number of excellent instructional tapes available, often sold with calls. Whatever you do, make sure that you recognise and can imitate the basic goose calls before you try them in a shooting situation, as many more geese are scared away from decoy patterns by a novice caller than he will manage to attract!

All calls used to be made out of wood, and many expert callers still prefer to use handcrafted wooden ones. However, plastic does have one major advantage in that the call is still effective when wet, where wooden calls sometimes fail. Naturally, you have to use the correct call for each species of goose, although there are some which claim to be able to imitate both greylags and pinkfeet, depending on how you hold them and blow.

How and When to Shoot

A goose right overhead at a height of 20 yards seems to fill the sky and also seems to be moving so slowly that it seems impossible to miss. But if you allow yourself to be complacent, miss you most certainly will! Geese are invariably moving faster than they look. That they seem to be moving slowly is an optical illusion caused by their large size and relatively large wings, which appear to beat at a rather ponderous rate. In reality, a goose flying steadily is probably travelling every bit as fast as a teal racing along at full speed.

The sheer size of a goose is also deceptive. The vital area is much smaller in relation to the overall outline than is the case with more familiar quarry such as duck and gamebirds, and it is a great mistake not to take careful aim at a particular spot on a goose. It is important to select one bird, particularly when large skeins seem to confuse the eye. It may seem impossible that a shot could pass between the birds, so close do they appear to be flying, but in reality there will be a good 2 or 3 yards between the wingtips of neighbouring birds.

Although as a rule geese tend to look much closer than they really are, a goose overhead will look much further away than one at similar range but flying close to the ground. It is extraordinary how convincing this illusion is, and I have often had people tell me that a goose passing over at a height of 30 yards is well out of range, when a goose landing among the decoys at 30 yards appears to be almost on the end of their barrels. I believe this has something to do with the lack of visual reference points when one is looking towards the sky, and the phenomenon is well known in game shooting, where a 35 yard pheasant looks stratospheric. The only solution to the problem of estimating range is experience and, once again, the familiar refrain – if in doubt for any reason whatsoever, do not shoot!

The best advice I have heard is to treat the goose's head like a snipe, concentrating one's aim on it and totally ignoring the rest of the body, in the hope that the shot pattern will be placed accurately and sufficiently far forward to give a clean kill.

After an initial shot has been fired, overhead geese will invariably climb steeply, which may allow a second shot at a target which requires much less lead and is therefore technically easier. Some Guns deliberately wait until others have fired for this reason.

Choosing the right moment to shoot can be difficult, especially when one is in a party of Guns. Obviously, it is necessary to wait until the birds are in range, but this in itself can be difficult to judge. Shooting at out-of-range geese is a grave infringement of etiquette, and all the more so when thoughtlessness spoils it for the others. Once again, if you have any doubts at all, then do not shoot, and you will not go too far wrong.

It is best if a single individual in the party is nominated to call the shots, but he must be able to see all around him. The classic error occurs when a single goose comes into the decoys and is shot at while, unbeknown to the person in charge, a skein of 20 is just approaching from another direction. The ideal situation is to let singletons and couples land if they are being followed by bigger groups. Having said this, geese are unpredictable, and I have lost count of the number of times I have held back from firing at a small bunch, only to see the bigger group disappear over the horizon minutes later.

You should allow committed geese to come right in to the decoys, but again this is fraught with uncertainties; once again, I have often held fire while geese circled in range, only for them to head off without coming any closer.

Geese may not necessarily depart the scene once they have been shot at. If you keep well hidden even when you shoot, and recommence calling immediately after you have fired and the birds have flared away, they will sometimes come back right over you, confused and unable to pinpoint the direction of the gunshots. I have a feeling that this applies particularly to first-year birds when one or more of the older birds in a family party has been shot. While I may be guilty of undue sentimentalism, I would not feel comfortable about calling birds back in these circumstances, although I readily admit that my attitude is based in emotion rather than logic. After all, it may be better to bag an entire family group rather than to disrupt it by bagging just one or two, and perhaps leaving inexperienced birds leaderless.

Driving

Driving geese is contentious. It almost always involves pushing them off their feeding grounds and this, together with the apparent ease and lack of skill or discomfort for the gunner, gives the whole business some of the less welcome connotations of driven game shooting. In fact, this is a little unfair, not least to driven game shooting, but then wild geese are accorded a status all their own.

There are two main situations in which driving may be justifiable: when geese are attracted to decoys but land too far away (this may have been deliberately engineered, of course, if the only cover is too far from the feeding area); and when there is a small group of geese that would otherwise be stalked. Both situations really only apply to the morning, because of the requirement for the geese to spend enough of the day feeding. On the whole, I think it is unacceptable to drive geese off their roosts in the morning, or to drive them off the feeding grounds in the evening.

The success of a drive hinges on getting the geese to fly over the Guns within range. This is always going to be a very chancy matter, although the odds narrow the closer one can get to the geese on the ground. Naturally, the Guns will have to be hidden.

Whoever is doing the driving should try to approach from a direction which will cause the geese to fly over the Guns. This direction of approach is not necessarily directly opposite the Guns, because of variable factors like the direction and strength of the wind, the easiest flightpath – which may be constrained by trees or hills – and the direction of the area the geese will wish to head for when disturbed. Probably the ideal scenario is to get the Guns within a couple of hundred yards of the geese, well concealed at a point where there is an obvious gap in a line of woods or tall trees, with the wind blowing straight through the gap from the Guns to the geese.

Conclusion

Whatever tactics you use, you will find that there is immense satisfaction in making plans which come to fruition, having drawn on all your knowledge of the quarry. There will be many other occasions when you are defeated. When it does all come together, however, please remember one principle above all others: restraint.

CHAPTER EIGHT

Somewhere to Shoot

If you want to shoot geese, then first find your geese. The encouraging fact is that there are now very few parts of Britain which are more than an easy drive away from an area which hosts quarry geese during at least some part of the shooting season. If you set about the task with real enthusiasm, you can find geese quietly hidden away in most likely places at certain times of the year and even, in the case of Canadas and resident or feral greylags, in some apparently unlikely places. Useful sources of information include the BASC, ornithological guidebooks, and the advice of fellow sportsmen – including anglers.

Finding geese is not necessarily a problem. Gaining permission to shoot them is a very different matter. In essence, there are three main ways of obtaining goose shooting: on the foreshore (public or club); inland, through the permission of the relevant authority; or with a professional goose guide. Access to the foreshore is severely restricted nowadays, even in Scotland, where much of the prime territory is either a non-shooting reserve or managed by a wildfowling club. This is probably just as well, but it can act as a barrier to the newcomer to either the sport or the locality. Many clubs offer day tickets or other means of short-term access, but in my experience they are not always very open about these schemes. It is best to contact the

BASC, who should be able to put you in touch with the right people. You can always apply to join a club, of course, but you may be faced by a depressingly long waiting list. On the other hand, you will find that it is a thoroughly worthwhile investment in time.

Inland shooting is, of course, totally restricted, and tends to be much more expensive.

One obvious source of goose shooting is the various sporting hotels and inns which offer to arrange a variety of shooting and fishing, often in conjunction with local guides and estates. A good, friendly, understanding hotel is an enormous help on a shooting trip, but working on the assumption that quality of shooting is the first priority, good accommodation can usually be found to fit in with one's plans, rather than the other way round.

By applying direct to major landowners (who are not necessarily individuals, but may be companies or trusts of various types) you may be able to negotiate some form of agreement. If the estate is keepered, the keeper will almost inevitably have a considerable say in the matter. The modern keeper is often a business manager in his own right, and by approaching him direct you may be able to negotiate terms. Otherwise, you should write to the estate manager at the estate office (which may be run by one of the big surveying firms) well *before* the season and politely put forward a tentative proposal, making it clear that you expect to pay a fee. Word process your letter and put it on headed paper (if you do not have any, get some made up). If the answer is anything other than a straightforward 'no', then you are effectively in the running, and should start to negotiate. In most cases, you would be best advised to put together a small party of Guns, so that you are regarded as a feasible commercial proposition by the estate.

Some estates prefer to take bookings through sporting agents – indeed, these agents may be commissioned to take full responsibility for managing the sporting assets of the estate. Some agents are highly professional and very helpful, while others have little real interest in goose shooting and will instead try to sell you all sorts of other shooting; all agents tend to be expensive, and they will almost invariably insist on putting together some form of package deal, both to gain maximum revenue for the estate (and themselves!) and also to keep control of your activities. This can work very well, but it does rob you of the ability to plan your own operations, which I always think is a major part of the enjoyment.

Another possibility is to rent the goose shooting rights to a particular patch of goose country, but this is a fairly major undertaking, although it may be very worthwhile if it allows you ready access. You will probably have to put together some form of syndicate, and even then the cost may be prohibitive. On the other hand, it can be a very fulfilling way of obtaining goose shooting, as it allows you to be the master of your own land.

You may still be lucky enough to strike a bargain on the spot with a land-owner or farmer, but the days when BB and his pals used to knock on the farmer's door in the almost sure hope of securing a shoot for the morning are long gone. Commercialism, the growth in the number of inland goose shooters, the advent of professional goose guides and worries about security have seen to that.

Almost all goose shooters employ the services of a guide at some stage. Indeed, this may be the only way for an individual Gun to obtain decent goose shooting, especially inland. A very small number of goose guides have been blamed for some of the worst excesses of over-commercialised shoot-ing, but it is important to realise that they are very much the exception. Most of the problems seem to have been caused by so-called guides who know little of the sport (and care even less) acquiescing to the demands of gunners who have little appreciation of the etiquette of sporting shooting of any sort, let alone goose shooting. Proper guides, on the other hand, have a long-term vested interest in curbing the behaviour of irresponsible so-called guides and clients alike; in general, they are a force for good in goose shooting.

The BASC estimated that there were about 35 goose guides in Britain in 1996, of whom 15 were registered with the BASC. Some general wild-fowling guides have been in business for many years, and have become well known figures to generations of fowlers. MacKenzie Thorpe, of the Wash, was immortalised in Colin Willock's book, *Kenzie the Wild-Goose Man*, while Bill Powell of the Solway was perhaps equally famous. In accounts of earlier years we hear of names such as Sam Bone of Wells, while well-known goose guides with whom I have shot in recent years include Alan Myers, Percy Betts and Alan Murray. There must be many more guides of good standing, and of course some of the very best are enthusiastic youngsters who are in the process of making their names.

For some reason, we like to believe that guides are invariably worthy indi-viduals, wise in the ways of fowl and fowlers, sage rustics steeped in the lore of weather, tides and moon states. On meeting these notable characters, we try to impress them with our decency and common sense, well aware that it is we who are being judged by them, rather than the other way round. Some guides have indeed dealt with literally hundreds of expectant goose shooters, they have helped countless novices to shoot their first goose, and they have spent hundreds or even thousands of hours out on the foreshore or in the fields. They have seen it all before, but they still do their very best to make each trip a memorable one.

Yet although there are many such guides who deserve instant respect, I have to say that in my experience, which includes using guides in most of the major goose haunts in Britain, there are a great many who are distressingly ordinary human beings. I am not saying they are all 'con-men' (although some are), just that all humans are different in character, knowledge, sense of humour, etc., and this applies to guides as much as to anybody. You can, therefore, find clashes of character.

For many, guiding is simply a business – no more, and no less. It is a means of earning money, and as such they want to gain the maximum return for the minimum effort. There is nothing intrinsically wrong with this, but you would be wise to pick a guide who has a real interest in geese. The problem is that for you, a week's goose shooting may be the highlight of your shooting year. You may have planned it months before and scrimped and saved for the cost. For the guide, however, it is just another week in a long season. Naturally, he would prefer you to go away happy and ready to spread the word, and it would be most convenient if you were to book a repeat trip – this boosts his reputation and leaves you to organise the party with minimal work or advertising on his part. But you must also realise that there are lots more clients where you came from – goose shooting has never been so popular. Some of the good guides are booked up well in advance of the season, and have clients who have been shooting with them for years. Others have to advertise heavily.

It is unlikely that many guides could make a living out of such a seasonal activity, so most guides have other jobs. Some work in related areas, such as gamekeeping or acting as a ghillie, but a great many are self-employed, doing a number of other jobs. I know of one who is a private detective, several who are publicans or hoteliers, a gunmaker and firearms dealer, a dog trainer . . . there are endless permutations. Many proprietors of sporting inns and hotels either act as guides or supply guides, with shooting guests providing a major source of occupancy and income during the winter.

Unfortunately, the variety of types of guide is matched by their variable quality. The demand for inland goose shooting is such that virtually anybody can set himself up as a guide, put a few ads in the sporting press or local gunshop windows (with a contra-deal, naturally) and sit back to take calls from eager clients. All too often, these clients partake once and never return, probably disillusioned with goose shooting for life.

Yet it is not always a case of unscrupulous so-called guides ripping-off clients. Most of the good guides will gleefully tell you horror stories of greedy or ignorant shooters. One guide I know always used to ban the use of anything larger than a 12-bore among his shooting parties because long experience had taught him that either someone with a big-bore would blaze away at incoming birds before the others had a chance or, equally likely, the others would accuse the heavy gunner of doing so. The end result was much the same, and many guides have tales of grown men fighting over a dead goose!

The question of whether guides should carry guns is, to my mind, very simple: of course they should, provided that they are used to help bag birds which are obviously hit but would otherwise escape. I suppose it is also acceptable for a guide to shoot on his own account, but I think that this should apply to very small parties and that the guide should in most cases wait until his clients have fired. Problems arise when the guide shoots before his clients get a chance.

In *My Wild Goose Chase*, Bill Powell records how he was once unfairly accused of always putting himself in the best spot when he was guiding two rather pompous individuals on the foreshore. In characteristic Powell fashion, he brooked no further nonsense from them. On that occasion, it seems that Powell's indignation was well justified, especially when one considers the element that chance invariably plays in success on the foreshore. But I have encountered less defensible behaviour among guides.

Once, in Cumbria, my party was promised a morning goose flight while staying at a well-known lodge for a few days' rough shooting. The lodge itself was very comfortable and hospitable. The young keeper, however, was a remarkably taciturn individual whose manner was brusque to the point of rudeness.

In due course, we found ourselves stumbling along behind this surly character in the grey light of dawn as he led us through a succession of marshy fields. We had no idea how far we were going, nor what the plan was. He apparently thought that we did not need to know. We just trotted after him as he strode along at a cracking pace without so much as a glance over his shoulder.

Suddenly, I spotted a single greylag afloat on a large splash in a stubble field. Grabbing the keeper by the arm, I whispered to him while pointing out the bird, which was some 80 yards away. Without further ado, the keeper whipped up his gun (which to my astonishment was loaded) and discharged both barrels at the hapless bird. Not surprisingly, it flew off unscathed. The keeper swore mightily – the most enthusiastic utterance we ever heard from him, incidentally – and reloaded as he recommenced his forced march, continuing to grumble under his breath. Our guns were still in their slips. Needless to say, we did not get a shot at a goose that morning.

On another occasion, near the Montrose basin in Scotland, we drove after a guide's estate car over a frozen track towards a place where he was going to line us out for an evening flight. The guide's car suddenly veered towards a small spinney and slowed down. Then it stopped, and we saw frantic activity in the back. To our astonishment, a gun barrel was then poked out of one of the rear windows, and pointed towards the spinney. Following the line of aim, we saw the silhouette of two long-tailed cock pheasants in a thorn bush. Two shots, and the two pheasants crashed to the ground through the twigs. Our guide dashed in to secure his booty, and stashed it under some decoys in the back of his car. He turned to us with a villainous grin and said: 'I've been after them all the season!' The incident was not mentioned again, and I have a feeling that we had unwittingly been involved in an act of brazen poaching.

When you employ a guide, you are paying for local knowledge and expertise. In the case of inland shooting, you are also paying for access to the land. Your money is supposed to ensure a contribution that you could not make yourself, so you need to be clear about what you think you are buying and how that relates to what the guide thinks he is selling. You might reasonably expect a competent guide to have a good idea of likely flight lines and to be fully knowledgeable about the geese in the district – where they roost and feed, how many there are, the mix of species and the likelihood of coming across protected species, how they tend to react to various weather conditions, and so forth. Your guide should supply all the decoys and at least some hide-building materials, show you the best cover for hides, and either carry out any calling himself or authorise others to do it as instructed. He should have full permission to take you shooting over the land, confirm that you are aware of prevailing laws or codes of conduct, and generally control proceedings. Lastly, he must carry full insurance.

For your part, you should be scrupulously punctual in arriving at your meeting place and have checked that you have all your kit and are properly clothed. On arrival at the field, you should help to put decoys out, lend a hand building hides and generally make yourself useful. Above all, you must do what you are told!

A guide cannot guarantee geese, of course, and it is unwise to judge his performance on the basis of just one or two flights. I have helped to set up flights when all the omens were excellent and our chief concern was where to buy more film for our cameras, as we were convinced we would have to stop shooting within minutes. In the event, we did not get a single shot! Geese are, after all, totally wild. The fields can be covered with them one day, and barren the next. A good guide generally spends a lot of time on reconnaissance, but you have to accept that all this does is to narrow the odds.

What the guide *can* control, however, is you. Many guides tell you when to shoot and when to stop. This can be very useful when there are novices, in mixed parties of shooters who do not know each other, or when the number and deployment of shooters is such that some form of central control is vital. With experienced shooters in small parties, however, it may be unnecessary. Personally, I do not like shooting with strangers because they are an unknown quantity in terms of safety and sporting etiquette. But some guides are greedy; the more shooters they can pack into a ditch in the morning, the more money they can collect. This can lead to extended parties being cobbled together in a manner that is unsatisfactory to every-one except the guide. If you have booked as a single Gun, it is almost inevitable that you will be asked to join a party. This is fair enough, but some guides seem to think they have the right to mix and match as they please, without even the courtesy of introducing people to each other, let alone asking permission. Yet ill-matched parties can spoil it for everybody.

Some guides do not like their Guns to be at all involved in the planning of a flight. I find this rather off-putting, as I do not like to be led to a ditch and told to get in and shut up until told to shoot – it is like stepping up to the shooting gallery at a travelling fair, and is not exactly a 'quality hunting experience', as the Americans would say. I recall once asking a well-known guide if I could come with him during his afternoon reconnoitre for geese. 'Why, don't you believe I've got any?' was his snarled response. He soon calmed down when he realised that I was genuinely interested, and he proved to be a very good guide. But the incident gave me a sad insight into how guides see their clients – which is probably an even sadder reflection on the average client.

There are certain guidelines it is worth following in selecting a guide for an inland goose shooting trip. First, try to put together your own party of shooters. This lessens the chances of being put with a bunch of unsavoury characters. Then you should ask around, and take the advice of people whose judgement you trust based on their *first-hand* experience of a partic-ular guide. I emphasise this because the world of goose shooting is as full of gossip, rumour and intrigue as the House of Commons. I have heard graphic tales of disgraceful behaviour from people who turn out not to have been present at the occasion but 'know somebody who was'. Even some of the best guides have a habit of hinting darkly at the antics of their competitors, although they take good care not to make specific claims in case somebody follows them up. Settle for nothing less than first-hand accounts from some-body you trust. Failing this, a good starting point would be to ring the BASC and ask for a contact list of registered guides.

Next, if you can, speak to the guide – either in person or over the tele-phone. Do not rely solely on letters, advertisements, brochures or booking forms, but engage in a frank and open discussion which runs according to your own agenda. All too often, we read or hear what we want, rather than remaining objective. Any good guide should be happy to chat to you. In addition to the normal queries about costs, accommodation and dates, you should make sure the conversation covers the following points:

1. Is he registered with the BASC? If not, why not? There must be good guides who are not registered, but I presume they have good reasons – in which case they will not mind telling you.

2. Does he abide by the BASC code of practice? Once again, the same considerations apply, although you should also check that he is covered by third-party insurance.

3. How does he charge? The norm is a fixed fee per person per flight, or an amount for the total, perhaps with a menu of other types of shooting. If he starts talking about an amount per goose shot you should be very cautious, as this opens the door to excessive bags. This sort of calculation is all very well with reared birds like pheasants, but it is generally inappropriate with wild geese, where it smacks of a numbers game rather than wild sport.

4. What size of party does he take? The important thing to establish is that he does not pack more people in without your permission. Of course, if you book in a party of six and turn up with only four without prior warning, he is entitled to make up the lost income, but he should still have the courtesy to inform you.

5. What sort of acreage does he have access to? You will be lucky to get a straight answer to this at this stage, but it might just flush out the so-called guides who do not actually have any guaranteed access at all, or who overshoot small acreages.

6. How long has he been operating as a guide? Length of service is no guarantee of competence, nor, conversely, is a newcomer automatically suspect. But it is another part of the overall picture which you can judge for yourself. Well-known and long-established guides tend to have access to good land and have reputations to maintain.

7. Will he accompany you at all times? Some established guides have assistants who help them out during the season. Sometimes these assistants are very good, but they are another variable factor. If your guide makes a habit of taking one party out himself while another is taken by his assistant, then he should be frank about it.

8. Lastly, have a general chat about geese. Does he sound knowledgeable about the geese in his district? Does he seem to care about them?

If I had been able (or willing!) to take my own advice and ask these basic questions in former years, I would have saved myself a great deal of fruitless wild goose chasing. As in so many aspects of life, one learns by experience. It is amazing how often even those of us who should know better can get caught out. I should emphasise that the problems are not only due to the few dishonest guides, but in many more cases to a mismatch between the expectations of the client and the intentions of the guide.

Percy Betts, a guide well-known in the Southwest of Scotland.

I well remember one trip I made on my own, near the end of a season, when I ignored every warning sign. My usual guides were all fully booked, but my eye was caught by an advertisement in a sporting magazine. I rang the number and found myself speaking to a pleasant woman (apparently the guide was out looking for geese, nor would he be available later).

'We never take more than eight Guns, and in your case it will be only four – two experienced Welsh fowlers who have been coming to the Solway for years, my husband, who will be guiding, and yourself,' the voice on the telephone assured me. 'We're very strict about following the code of practice.' I duly ended up at a distinctly superior B & B in a small town in southwest Scotland. The guide was a pleasant young Englishman who had moved north several years before.

I met my two Welsh colleagues at some unearthly hour the next morning, as we piled into the guide's jeep amidst a clutter of guns and decoys. Off we set, towards the flat grassland bordering Wigtown Bay. To my surprise, we stopped at a small cottage on the way. It appeared that we were being joined by another guide and his party of two friends from Oxfordshire, who turned up ten minutes later in a Range Rover.

After leaving the cars and splashing down a muddy lane, we scrambled over the inevitable barbed wire fence and laid out a dozen decoys. They

Alan Murray – one of Britain's fore-most goose guides.

looked rather lonely on the huge grass field. The second guide, who had not been introduced to us, exuded great bonhomie and confidence. 'They'll come from over there,' he proclaimed, jabbing a finger towards the sea, 'and then swing round to the decoys to drop in here, giving you all a good chance.' We lined out in a ditch, with me at one end.

Dawn arrived, and sure enough a few skeins of pinkfeet appeared – although from inland, rather than the sea. Unfortunately, they were deter-mined to drop into a neighbouring field. We only had permission for the particular field that we were in, so there was no point in moving. Later two greylags swept in unexpectedly from my side. I waited until they were well in range, then raised my gun. Then two shots rang out from further up the ditch. The geese, untouched, flicked away downwind. Recovering from my shock, I hastily poked at the departing geese and fired – and missed!

My next chance came when a single greylag floated directly over my head, not 30 yards up. I fired one barrel, and the goose collapsed. As it did so, I heard another shot from further up the line. Cheerful Charlie appeared and purloined the goose. 'One up to my boys!' he crowed, as he passed by me, swinging the goose. I presumed that we had both fired at the same time.

It was only when we packed up that we discovered that we had been joined at some stage by three other Guns, uniformly clad in balaclavas. Cheerful Charlie seemed to know them and greeted them jovially; no doubt his morning's takings had just soared.

We had booked a duck flight that night, and were careful to be ready on time. Once again, however, we stopped off *en route*. After an interminable wait, Cheerful Charlie turned up with the Oxford group, happily waving a can of lager at us through the window of the car. He led us to a likely looking pool and put us in position. We waited – and nothing happened. Eventually, when it was pitch black, we stumbled back to the cars in silence.

The next morning we went to the field adjoining our first site. In addition to the previous morning's group, there was one more person with the men in balaclavas, bringing the total to eleven Guns (including the guides). Could anything approach our decoys and escape unscathed?

Dawn arrived, but not many geese. The previous day's pinkfeet were nowhere to be seen. Eventually, a solitary greylag came in to the decoys, and was neatly felled with a single shot at 45 yards by one of the anonymous balaclava wearers. Then we saw a skein in the distance heading straight for us along the course of the river, breasting the stiff northerly breeze.

Inexorably closer and lower they came, as if drawn on a string. They were setting their wings. As they crossed a tall blackthorn hedge two fields away which marked the edge of the merse, at a height of perhaps 75 yards, we suddenly saw them swing sharply upwards. It is only when one sees them from such an angle that one realises how they can climb 10 or more yards in a second or two, standing on their tails and scooping the wind under their great wings. We heard a distant spatter of gunshots, indicating the cause of the disruption. We packed up in disgust as the geese departed in the direction they had come from.

That night, our guide boosted our morale with hints that we were going to a particularly choice flightpond. Best of all, there would only be the four of us. 'There are only three hides, but two of you won't mind sharing one,' he said. Indeed not, we assured him, full of team spirit and good humour.

However, once again we stopped off on the way, and waited. This time, Cheerful Charlie had brought a whole convoy with him. The sinister men in balaclavas were nowhere to be seen, but in their place was a whole van load of lads from Yorkshire. Together with the Oxford group, we numbered eleven again – including the guides.

We arrived *en masse* at the famous pool. It seemed to be about the size of my drawing room, so at least I would be somewhere near the centre of the action, I consoled myself. For a horrible moment it looked as though we were going to surround the pond, but then they decided to line us out along just one side. I was very relieved but, inevitably, I was still put at the end of the line, sharing a rudimentary hide with one of the Yorkshire group.

We waited. 'We were told there would only be the four of us here tonight,' said the Yorkshire lad, in a mildly accusative tone

'Same here,' I retorted.

He became friendlier as we swapped tales. Then we fell silent and stared out across the puddle of water, comrades in the face of adversity. Eventually, eight wigeon materialised over the centre of the pool. There seemed to be a moment of startled silence, and then the whole of one side of the pool erupted in gunfire; it was like the opening barrage at the battle of El Alamein – in fact, I think I heard someone shout 'Fire'! For an awful moment, it looked as though the object was to keep the wretched duck in the air, like a ping-pong ball on a jet of water. Later, a few more small groups of duck came in, to be greeted with equal enthusiasm.

If we had added up what everybody said they had shot, the bag would have been in double figures, but the dog only picked one wigeon and one teal; we probably all shot the same duck. If there were any others (which I doubt) they probably sank with the weight of the pellets.

However, the prospects for the next morning's goose flight really did look good. Our guide had actually been rung up by a farmer and asked to clear the geese, which had descended in their thousands on winter barley.

In response to a bit of gentle goading, the guide growled: 'This is my ground this time, and I'll sort everything out.' Later, after supper, I lost the toss and had to ask him how many Guns were coming out tomorrow. 'Oh, just six,' he replied, 'but you lot will take priority.' I reported back and we had an extra pint to celebrate.

The next morning, we were up particularly early. But once again, we had to wait for the others. 'I'm giving them till 6.30,' announced our guide, his jaw jutting, 'and then we're leaving, no matter what.' At 6.38 the rest of the convoy joined us, and we set off at breakneck speed. On arrival, I discovered that Cheerful Charlie had surpassed himself; I counted no less than 14 people piling out of the cars.

The platoon of bulkily clad fowlers squelched and rustled across the field. We rambled to a halt, bumping into each other in the stormy pre-dawn darkness. Our guide and Cheerful Charlie began a fervent whispered conversation. Then Cheerful Charlie began ladling out instructions to the assembled company. Our guide was silently acquiescent as we were led away to line out along a stone wall. The Welshmen muttered mutinously.

As Cheerful Charlie came down the line, adjusting people's positions, I pulled my balaclava down and prayed that he would not recognise me. Not a chance. 'Do you want to go down to the far corner of the field to practice some high overhead shots?' he said. I decided that the time had come to make a stand. Our guide was nowhere to be seen. My companions were egging me on. All popular uprisings need a leader.

'No,' I said quietly but firmly. Nobody spoke for a minute. The wind howled eerily. Emboldened, I followed up with a masterstroke: 'By the way, how many Guns are supposed to be out today – do we have enough guides?'

But Cheerful Charlie had dealt with barrack-room lawyers before. 'There are only ten Guns out – the rest are all guides,' he chuckled. 'Now hurry up, the others are waiting.' Deflated, I stumbled off as directed, followed by the crestfallen Welshmen.

That morning the pinkfeet arrived in armies, and kept on coming – skein after skein of them. Fortunately, we did not shoot too many. The Welshmen downed two or three, one of which was picked by the Balaclava Boys. I missed some spectacularly easy shots, but accounted for two geese.

I watched one small skein approach the Welshmen. As the geese came within range, there was a sudden volley of shots – not from them, but from the Balaclava Boys, who were 80 or so yards away! There were no other geese anywhere near at the time. For a moment I thought the Welshmen were going to return fire. The guides sat and did nothing. By this time there were people running all around the field, picking birds, blowing goose calls, and generally causing mayhem.

While the geese were still coming in the Balaclava Boys suddenly departed – allegedly with an ill-gotten goose secreted about their persons.

After breakfast I said my goodbyes and paid my bill. As I departed, I overheard the Welshmen chattering hopefully; it seemed they had been promised a good goose flight the next morning, and it was definitely only them and the guide . . .

I am aware that this story may give a rather jaundiced view of goose guides, but I reiterate the sentiments I expressed earlier – that the vast majority are thoroughly decent, reliable and responsible individuals who work hard for their money and provide a very worthwhile service.

If you are able to organise your own goose shooting, then you have only yourself to blame if it all goes wrong. Conversely, if you have directed operations which turn out to be successful, then the sense of fulfilment is all the greater. It is a pity that opportunities for private, *ad hoc* goose-shooting are now so rare, but they still exist in some regions, especially those where the farmers are not routinely pestered by hopeful goose shooters.

Driving home one January afternoon after a Scottish goose-shooting trip, I saw a gaggle of greylags feeding on new grass in Northumberland, not 25 miles from my home. As I was nearing the end of a 400 mile round trip, the irony was not lost on me. I decided there and then to track down the farmer – he could only say no, after all.

Night had fallen by the time I found myself running the inevitable gauntlet of assorted toothy terriers and neurotic collies in the farmyard. The farmer was a wiry, tough-looking elderly man. He and his wife were having tea by the television. I felt awkward as I explained my business. 'I was driving past you new grass on the bank, and I noticed a lot of geese giving it a hammering. I was wondering if you'd let me try to shoot a few? It'll just be me.'

He was hard of hearing, so I had to repeat it all over again. I felt foolish. He rubbed his chin for a moment, then said, 'Aye, well, it's all reet by me. They eat a canny bit o' grass, them things.' I thanked him profusely, then bolted.

The next morning I was awake before the alarm. After gulping some scalding coffee while the car defrosted I set off. It was bitterly cold with an icy, gusting easterly wind. The sky was mostly clear, and the stars looked like diamond dust thrown on a jeweller's black velvet cloth. As I left town the headlights began to illuminate wisps of dry, powdery snow being blown along the road in twisting snakes. I reached my destination 40 minutes before sunrise, but as I doused the lights I realised that the stars were already growing faint. I quickly unloaded all my gear and hurried off down the ankle-twisting ruts of a farm track, the cat-ice on the puddles crackling underfoot.

I was anxious about finding a good position for a hide at the bottom of the field, where a rickety wire fence marked the boundary between the sown grass and the rough pasture beyond. Almost immediately, however, I found an ideal site, where some boulders had been moved off the fields and piled in a corner. The only snag was that this was at the opposite side of the field to where the geese had been. I decided to set the decoys 70 yards upwind of the hide, in the hope that as the geese headed for their patch, flying into the wind, they would divert to look at the decoys and so pass directly over me.

I set to work with some urgency and rapidly discovered that I could not push the decoy pegs – essential in the stiff breeze – even an inch into the frozen ground. Frantically, I searched for the hammer which had, of course, worked its way right to the bottom of the bag. Just as it became light enough to work without a torch, the last decoy was set. I found I was sweating, despite the frigid air.

Having loaded two heavy brass cartridges into the eight-bore and laid it down carefully, I sat down in the boulders to catch my breath and have a cup of coffee. Greylags often flight quite late. But just as I reached for my flask, I heard the spine-tingling sound of distant geese. They were on the move!

I sat up. Suddenly, I heard a single, soft croak, quite distinct from the faraway goose gabble. I turned my head slightly, and froze – a dozen geese were coming straight for me!

Resisting the impulse to put my gun up, I forced myself to reach out for it slowly, without taking my eyes off the geese. They were only 25 yards high, and when they saw the decoys they set their wings and broke out into a burst of cackling which set my pulse racing.

I had the great gun in my hands, and cranked back the hammers. The geese started to beat their wings again as they crossed the fence 40 yards away. They looked much closer in the cold, clear atmosphere, but I held my fire, hugging the gun as I turned with them; they would come round again, closer.

But they did not! To my dismay, they wheeled away from the decoys and started to slide off towards the far side of the field. Panic and indecision. I jabbed the gun at the departing birds. If they went down over there, my decoys would never be able to compete. Should I shoot? I did, with both barrels.

The double crash shattered the morning air, sounding appallingly loud. I cowered. The geese powered up and away, shouting for all the world to hear. I half expected doors and windows to fly open at the cottages across the valley. Not a single goose so much as faltered. They were probably 45 yards away when I decided to fire, and at 30 mph (48 kph) the range would have been lengthening at about 15 yards a second, so my hesitation killed any remaining chance. In fact, it was an utterly stupid shot. I was furious with myself as I reloaded.

More geese were coming in, off to my right, by the sound of them, although I could not actually see them from my cramped position. The noise level fluctuated – they must be circling, probably puzzled by the behaviour of the first lot. Then the noise became louder and somehow more purposeful. Suddenly they burst into view, well over 100, in four or five ragged clumps, one behind the other. They were going to take the same line over the fence as the first lot. Should I move? Too late. Where was my goose call? No point; think!

Slowly, with forced and entirely false calmness, I laid another long cartridge on a tuft of frozen grass, base angled towards me. If I did get a shot, there would not be time to reload two barrels.

The leading geese saw the decoys. Their calling intensified, and then they altered course, pulling the succeeding skeins around with them. The whole lot were going to come straight over me at a height of less than 30 yards!

The first birds loomed over me on set wings. Despite the deafening clamour I could distinctly hear the air rattling their great pinions. I steeled myself to let the leaders pass right over, committing the whole lot.

This was it. Everything seems to slow down and become quiet as I hoisted the mighty 39-inch barrels skywards and tracked the muzzles along the outstretched neck of a goose, then pulled a bit further in front and . . .

Whoomph! I knew I had got it even before I saw it crumple. I switched to another with surprisingly calm efficiency. A mass of threshing wings obscured the sky above me as the great birds stood on their tails – impossible to miss. I barely bothered to aim. Whoomph! I stared in disbelief as the geese flew on, unscathed. A colossal thump as my first bird whacked into the iron ground jolted me back to reality.

I yanked the top lever across and pulled out two hot, smoking cartridges. They clanged onto the frozen ground like spent howitzer shells. The geese were almost out of range as I put the cartridge into the right barrel, thumbed back the hammer and picked what seemed to be the nearest goose. Whoomph! The goose was flailing the air. Another miss? No, he was foundering. Then he collapsed in mid-air and plummeted to the ground head first, wings folded like a huge falcon stooping. On impact the powder snow sprayed up like a shell burst.

The shrill clamour faded and I noticed that I was gasping to breathe through my clammy balaclava. I hastily pulled it off and the freezing air stung my damp face. All seemed uncannily quiet as I emerged cautiously from my hide, like an infantryman coming out of a foxhole.

After a couple of anxious minutes, I found the distant fallen goose. He was stone dead, lying on his back, with his white underparts blending with the frost and light snow.

I carefully laid both geese on the bank which formed the back of the hide, then poured a cup of coffee from the flask with a slightly unsteady hand. Glancing at my watch, I found that the action of this short flight had taken place over something less than four minutes.

CHAPTER NINE

The Way Forward

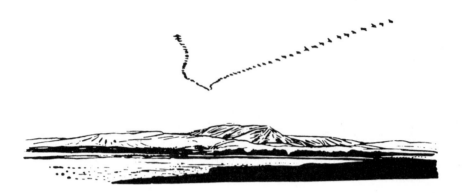

If geese were the sole consideration in the future of goose shooting, then we would have little to worry about. As we have seen, most quarry goose populations are currently in a very healthy state and, barring an environmental disaster on an almost unimaginable scale, none is likely to become threatened. The degradation of habitat has been halted (and even reversed in a few instances), breeding grounds are steadily becoming inviolable, and enlightened attitudes towards the harvesting of geese have all had a beneficial effect.

Unfortunately, the situation is not that simple. The future of goose shooting as a sport is inextricably linked to that of wildfowling, and through that to shooting in general, then beyond shooting to the whole issue of field sports. This is an area where our society shows deep divisions.

The automatic reaction of many people is that shooting is cruel. This is illogical, given that shooting is also held to be one of the most humane ways of killing an animal. Conservation groups often use shooting to control pest species. It seems that the matter of animal *welfare* is often confused with animal *rights*. In other words, when people say that shooting is cruel, what they really mean is that killing an animal for sport is cruel, in the sense that it is unnecessary and uncivilised. What really seems to offend people is the thought that those of us who shoot are doing so because we enjoy it. This charge of killing for fun is a gross oversimplification, and shows the fundamental hypocrisy of society.

As a society, we readily condone the rearing and slaughter of animals for meat (even if many of us prefer other people to do the actual killing, which must be a form of moral cowardice). We eat meat because it is a healthy, traditional food, and the ritual of preparing and eating it is an enjoyable, fulfilling experience. Meat is a food of choice, rather than necessity, but there is nothing wrong with that. Nobody eats meat because they enjoy the thought of killing – they simply do not see killing as wrong in this context.

Nor does the wildfowler, who enjoys trying to harvest a traditional, highly palatable quarry in a manner which involves considerable skill, knowledge, fieldcraft and physical exercise in the great outdoors. Thus the traditional turkey (or goose) dinner at Christmas is connected no more and no less to the fun of killing a bird than is the equally traditional Boxing Day shoot. The only difference I can see is that the shot bird will have enjoyed a truly free-range existence before being killed and eaten (you cannot get more free-range than from Iceland to Scotland and back!).

There is, of course, the question of wounding. But any wounding that does occur is inadvertent, and for most of us it actually detracts from the enjoyment of the overall experience. I have never met a wildfowler who takes pleasure in wounding a duck or goose – quite the reverse, in fact. Sporting etiquette dictates that one should do everything possible to minimise wounding, and most wildfowlers make strenuous efforts to retrieve wounded birds. This is not mere window dressing, because these people go to such efforts when there is nobody else present, nobody to impress. In addition, as we have seen, the inadvertent wounding of a goose by shooting seems to cause it relatively little distress. We should be very wary of ascribing human powers of emotion and reasoning to animals.

I do not think the charge that shooting is cruel stands up to scrutiny, but the issue of animal rights is much more complex. In a strict sense, animals cannot have 'rights', because the whole concept of rights is an entirely artificial creation which is only really applicable to humans who can reciprocate. But we have to accept that sentiment and emotion are the very stuff of human identity, so it is unwise to dismiss animal rights on technical grounds.

One of the problems facing the animal rights lobby is deciding where to draw the line. Their public pronouncements are often much more moderate than the hard-edged reality of their hidden agenda. I wonder how many well-meaning people who give money to these organisations realise that there is an underlying goal to phase out pets, on the basis that these animals are actually slaves? How many understand that the animal-rights case against shooting is just as applicable to horse racing, and fishing – particularly in the case of catch-and-release?

As a keen fisherman, I accept the overwhelming similarities between fishing and shooting. If we simply wanted to kill trout – or geese – there are much more convenient ways of doing so than using an artificial fly or a shotgun. After all, it is perfectly legal to shoot sitting geese at 200 yards with a rifle, but we do not – any more than we use a worm on chalk-stream trout.

As public concern about animal welfare grows, the abolitionists forecast the inevitable demise of shooting on the grounds that society no longer accepts cruel sports like cock-fighting, and time is also running out for shooting. Yet cock-fighting was banned more than 150 years ago, while Britain's shooting community is thriving. There is a clear distinction between a field sport and a barbaric practice like cock-fighting. In a field sport, the outcome is uncertain; the animal is in its natural environment and capable of using all its attributes to evade capture or death. Success depends almost entirely on the hunter's skill, physical prowess and knowledge – and the inevitable element of chance. The animal's death is as humane as the hunter can manage. With all but pest species, the carcase is used for food. Thus the killing of the quarry is a means to an end, rather than an end in itself. The motive is spiritual and emotional.

A despicable activity like cock-fighting, on the other hand, differs to this in almost every aspect, with financial greed in the form of gambling being the main motive.

Abolitionists sometimes talk about 'bloodlust', but this is an emotive and misleading term. Humans are hunters by instinct, evolution and tradition. There is nothing uncivilised about hunting – in fact, it has always been one of the great civilising forces, with its connotations of co-operation and codes of conduct. Abolitionists say that there is nothing intrinsically worthy about instinct, that some of our instincts are deeply antisocial in a modern context. In this narrow sense, I have to agree. But who is to say which instincts are acceptable, and which are not? Wildfowling's conventions have evolved in step with society, with attendant codes of behaviour concerning safety, respect for the quarry and conservation. Yet we cannot escape from the fact that our activities offend some people. On the other hand, such people also offend us, so who is being antisocial to whom?

In the final analysis, the argument seems to revolve around equally valid personal opinions, with pure logic being on the side of the hunter, and knee-jerk sentiment on the side of the abolitionists. However, there is one key distinction: we do not try to impose our will on the abolitionists, whereas they use every means possible to impose their will on us. We are defending our cultural heritage, they are attacking it (supposedly on behalf of animals). The sheer arrogance, self-righteousness and blind intolerance of some abolitionists is truly antisocial.

While I do not doubt that many abolitionists are fundamentally decent people, it seems to me that many are not really *for* animals, so much as *against* certain people. In this sense, they are a negative force in society. They do not build or persuade so much as destroy and demand. Unlike shooters and professional conservationists (who may or may not be anti-shooting) fervent abolitionists never seem to dig flightponds, plant trees, or improve habitat in any meaningful way. Their actions are merely disruptive.

Yet it is not just attitudes at home which may cause us problems. Legislation drafted in dusty offices hundreds of miles away in foreign countries, and the seemingly inexorable move to rationalise hunting regulations across countries with widely varying sporting traditions and circumstances, are likely to hinder our freedom to take responsibility for our own actions.

Nothing is more depressing than believing that a deteriorating situation is both unfair and out of control, where one cannot do anything to influence the outcome, and simply has to shrug one's shoulders and make the best of things. I suspect that this is the case with many wildfowlers, who are deeply suspicious of the real motives of the green lobby – a powerful, pervasive group which (with exquisite irony) has replaced the multinational corporations as the great international wheelers and dealers whom nobody can afford to offend.

To some wildfowlers, the army of professional conservationists (or 'protectionists') make a convenient enemy. In an age where arguments and viewpoints are distilled into easily-digestible soundbites to be fed to an overwhelmingly urban population, the relationship between hunter and hunted is difficult to explain. Urbanites tend to think of artificial games as sport. They may see the whole concept of field sports and associated sporting ethics as a rather disgraceful application of the principles of fair play to what they term 'blood sports'. This view is shared by some conservationists, most of whom – by sheer statistical probability – live in built-up landscapes.

All too often, shooters are forced to defend themselves on the basis that they too are conservationists. There is much truth in this, of course. After all, shooting as a sport depends upon harvesting a sustainable crop, just as forestry entails chopping down some trees and planting others. Nobody in their right mind would accuse a forester of being 'against trees', any more than anyone should think that a wildfowler is against wildfowl.

But let us face the fact that conservation is a practical consequence of well-managed shooting, rather than the objective. We do not go shooting to conserve wetlands any more than we eat beef to preserve pasture. When the level of argument is raised above the level of the slanging match, we have some good points to make. The problem is getting the argument to this level in the first place. As it is, an opinion poll asking the simple question 'Do you agree that shooting for sport is cruel?' is bound to receive a wholly predictable response. This is why this device is so often used by the abolitionists. They never ask an equally shallow question which could get an unhelpful answer, such as 'Do you believe that eating meat should be made a criminal offence?'

Given the enormous, unassailable power of the conservation lobby, we shooters are Greeks to their Romans, but this is not to say that we no longer have a valid place in society. Sadly, conservationists all too often fail to exercise power with responsibility and respect for fellow humans. While many informed conservationists acknowledge the spin-off conservation benefits of sporting shooting, some cannot accept that true conservation can happen on anything other than their own terms. They expect – indeed, demand – that their pet conservation projects be paid for out of taxpayers' money, giving them sole access to ornithological playgrounds uncluttered by 'unnecessary' things like farmers, foresters or wildfowlers.

Wildfowl protectionists are fond of pointing out that many people can enjoy the sight and sound of a living wild goose, while only one person can enjoy the process involved in bagging it. Like all the most plausible propaganda, this claim has an element of truth. But it is deeply flawed. It takes no account of quantum, for one thing. Just how many geese do we need for the enjoyment of one group of people, before allowing another group to take a small, easily sustainable harvest? There is an almost Orwellian ring to the birdwatcher's mantra: 'One hundred thousand geese good, two hundred thousand geese better.' To descend to an equally simplistic illustration, most people could not even spot the difference between a flock of 100 greylags and one of 90, yet that difference represents the wildfowlers' share over a season. If quarry goose populations fell and stabilised at their 1950s levels, would we still be allowed to shoot them, as Peter Scott did?

Many wildfowlers believe that dealing with the conservation lobby is a one-way street; we give, and they take. What conceivable conservation rationale was there for removing the curlew from the quarry list? And why has the brent not been returned to the list? Why the restrictions on lead shot, when lead poisoning is barely a problem in this country?

Yet I have little sympathy with some of these attitudes. The fact is that a grouse-shooting peer was instrumental in removing the curlew from the list, while the brent goose issue is now tied up in European red tape and we should not expect the conservation organisations to fight our case for us. As for lead shot, we cannot expect our claims to have a concern for the environment to be taken seriously while sprinkling tons of an unarguably toxic substance over sensitive wetland areas.

We wildfowlers should join forces with the conservationists to protect habitat and wildfowl species, while educating these people about the real nature of our sport, and trying to blunt their self-righteousness wherever it appears.

As things are, we have little real cause to complain. We have already seen that we have more geese to shoot at than ever before, yet what did we do to deserve such a cornucopia? The example of the 1967 amendment banning the sale or barter of dead wild geese stands as a shining star in an otherwise rather dark firmament. The 'small bag' philosophy was promulgated by writers like BB long before any shooting organisation took a formal stance on this issue, and overshooting was a factor in the decline of some quarry goose species. If it was not for organisations like the WWT, how would geese be faring today? Of course, many wildfowlers are members of the WWT, while individual clubs and the BASC are doing sterling work. But we need to give them more support. At present, only about one sixth of Britain's shooters are members of the BASC, whereas virtually every keen birdwatcher is a member of the RSPB.

We still do not invest enough in our sport, unlike the Americans who have given us a wonderful example in the form of Ducks Unlimited – an organisation funded by waterfowlers which wields unrivalled power in the field of North American wildfowl conservation.

We still expect others to understand and appreciate our point of view without the need to explain, and we retire muttering darkly to ourselves about the unfairness of it all when we do not get our own way. What have you done for your sport recently? When was the last time you took a young-ster shooting, or talked about wildfowling to a non-shooting friend? Are you making your voice heard in various conservation organisations? In the final analysis, people try to judge issues for themselves, and in this direct experience and personal contact exert a powerful influence. If every one of Britain's live quarry shooters converted just a few friends or relatives to no more than an understanding of shooting, the political threat to the sport would be ineffectual.

The conservationists want information on total annual bags to help manage international wildfowl populations more effectively. We should do our best to provide such factual information, because the very last thing we want is to place too much pressure on a quarry species, let alone be accused of endangering a species. Without accurate information, we are leaving too much to chance, and relying far too much on those who do not have the interests of our sport at heart, even if they are not actually anti-shooting. The conservationists need more money for habitat protection and creation. We should help them raise it, so that we also have a stake in these projects.

Unnecessary regulation of our sport would be regrettable. The unreasonable restriction of goose shooting would be a disaster. But the collapse of a quarry goose population would be an absolute catastrophe, bringing the sport down with it. As long as we get our priorities in order, the future of goose shooting should be assured.

Appendix A: Sunrise/Sunset Times at Popular Goose Shooting Stations

		Sep 1	Sep 15	Oct 1	Oct 15	Nov 1	Nov 15	Dec 1	Dec 15	Jan 1	Jan 15
King's Lynn:	Rise	06.08	06.32	06.59	07.24	06.55	07.21	07.47	08.04	08.10	08.03
	Set	19.47	19.14	18.36	18.04	16.28	16.05	15.47	15.43	15.54	16.13
Southport:	Rise	06.21	06.45	07.14	07.39	07.12	07.38	08.06	08.23	08.29	08.21
	Set	20.02	19.29	18.49	18.16	16.39	16.14	15.56	15.52	16.02	16.22
Newton Stewart:	Rise	06.24	06.50	07.20	07.48	07.22	07.50	08.20	08.37	08.44	08.35
	Set	20.11	19.35	18.54	18.19	16.40	16.14	15.54	15.49	16.00	16.21
Kinross:	Rise	06.17	06.45	07.17	07.45	07.21	07.51	08.22	08.41	08.47	08.37
	Set	20.09	19.32	18.49	18.13	16.32	16.05	15.43	15.37	15.48	16.10
Forfar:	Rise	06.14	06.42	07.15	07.44	07.21	07.51	08.22	08.41	08.47	08.37
	Set	20.07	19.30	18.47	18.10	16.29	16.01	15.39	15.32	15.43	16.06
Peterhead:	Rise	06.08	06.37	07.11	07.41	07.19	07.51	08.23	08.43	08.49	08.38
	Set	20.05	19.26	18.41	18.04	16.21	15.52	15.28	15.21	15.33	15.56
Inverness:	Rise	06.18	06.47	07.21	07.51	07.29	08.01	08.33	08.53	08.58	08.47
	Set	20.15	19.36	18.51	18.14	16.31	16.02	15.39	15.32	15.43	16.06

Note: These times are in BST up to and including Oct 15, and in GMT (one hour later than BST) from Nov 1.

Reproduced, with permission, from data supplied by HM Nautical Almanac Office. Copyright Particle Physics and Astronomy Research Council.

Appendix B: References and Recommended Reading

References:

BB (Denys Watkins-Pitchford). *Tide's Ending.* Hollis & Carter, 1950.

Begbie, Eric. *The New Wildfowler* (editor, third edition). Stanley Paul, 1989.

Cadman, Arthur. *Tales of a Wildfowler.* Collins, 1957.

Douglas, James. *The Sporting Gun.* David & Charles, 1983.

Duncan, Stanley (with Thorne, Guy.) *The Complete Wildfowler.* Grant Richards, 1911.

Thomas, Gough (G T Garwood). *Gough Thomas's Gun Book.* A & C Black, 1969.
'Guns and Cartridges', *The New Wildfowler in the 1970s.* Barrie & Jenkins, 1970.

Hardy, D E. 'Observations on the Pinkfooted Goose in Central Iceland, 1966', *Wildfowl.*

Hawker, Lieutenant-Colonel Peter. *Instructions to Young Sportsmen.* Longmans, 1814.

Humphries, John. 'The Killing Fields', *Shooting Times and Country Magazine,* 1993.

Marchington, John. *The History of Wildfowling.* A & C Black, 1980.
The Practical Wildfowler. A & C Black, 1977.

McDougall, Douglas. *Goose Fever.* Private, 1972.
8-Bore Ammunition. Private, 1985.

Owen, Myrfyn. *Wild Geese of the World.* B T Batsford, 1980.
Wildfowl in Great Britain (editor, second edition). Cambridge University Press, 1986.

Payne-Gallwey, Sir Ralph. *High Pheasants in Theory and Practice.* Longmans, 1913.

Pitman, Ian. *And Clouds Flying.* Faber, 1947.

Powell, Bill. *The Grey Geese Call.* Herbert Jenkins, 1956.
My Wild Goose Chase. Herbert Jenkins, 1954.

Reiger, George. *The Wildfowler's Quest.* Lyons & Burford (USA), 1989.

Savory, Alan. *Norfolk Fowler.* Geoffrey Bles, 1953.

Sedgewick, Noel. 'Inland Marsh Shooting', *The New Wildfowler,* Stanley Paul, 1989.

Scott, Sir Peter. *Morning Flight.* Country Life, 1935.
The Eye of the Wind. Hodder & Stoughton, 1961.
Wild Geese and Eskimos. Country Life, 1951.

Swan, Mike. *Fowling for Duck.* Crowood, 1988.

Thorneycroft, Nigel. *Fowler's Moon.* George Harrap, 1955.

Wentworth Day, James. *The Modern Fowler*. Batchworth, 1934.
White, T H. *England Have My Bones*. Collins, 1936.
Willock, Colin. *Kenzie the Wild-goose Man*. Andre Deutsch, 1962.

Recommended reading (in addition to the above):

BB. *Dark Estuary*. Hollis & Carter, 1953. Very much in the same vein as *Tide's Ending*.

Manka the Sky Gypsy. Eyre & Spottiswode, 1939. The story of a white Pinkfoot. Interestingly, BB has Manka breeding in Spitsbergen; not until the 1950s would it become certain that our Pinkfeet come from Iceland, with Spitsbergen hosting a discrete population.

Recollections of a Longshore Gunner. The Boydell Press, 1976. A slim book, but still vintage BB.

Cadieux, Charles L. *Goose Hunting*. Stone Wall Press (USA) 1979. An account of goose shooting in America, where conditions and regulations are very different to ours, though 'waterfowlers' and wildfowlers obviously share similar enthusiasms.

Kear, Dr Janet. *Man and Wildfowl*. T & AD Poyser, 1990. A thorough examination of our interaction with wildfowl through the ages. Informative and very readable, even if the author does seem biased against wildfowling.

Lorenz, Konrad. *The Year of the Greylag Goose*. UK edition by Eyre & Methuen, 1979. The author describes an astonishing range of behaviour and communication among a group of greylags studied in Austria. Superb photography.

Scott, Peter (with Fisher, James). *A Thousand Geese*. Collins, 1953. A diary account of Peter Scott's expedition to Iceland in 1951 where he discovered the main breeding grounds of our Pinkfeet.

Appendix C: Useful Addresses

BASC
Marford Mill
Rossett
Clwyd
LL12 0HL

BASC Scottish Centre
Trochry
Dunkeld
Tayside
PH8 0DY

BFSS
59 Kennington Road
London
SE1 7PZ

The Game Conservancy Trust
Fordingbridge
Hampshire
SP6 1EF

The Wildfowl & Wetlands Trust
Slimbridge
Gloucestershire
GL2 7BT

RSPB
The Lodge
Sandy
Bedfordshire
SG19 2DL

Appendix D: British Goose Survey figures

The various populations are ranked according to their current population status in Britain

Species	Breeding grounds	1950 (estimate)	Recent count	Peak count
Pinkfooted	Iceland/Greenland	30,000	200,000 (1995)	266,000(1994)
Brent	Russia	13,000	104,000 (1995)	124,000 (1991)
Greylag	Iceland	30,000	83,000 (1995)	115,000 (1990)
Canada	Britain (introduced)	2,600–3,600 (1953)	63,000 (1991)	–
Barnacle	Greenland	8,000	30,200 (1994)	–
Whitefronted	Greenland	2,500–4,500	19,250 (1994)	30,200 (1990)
Greylag	Britain (reintroduced)	1,000 ?	19,000 (1991)	22,000 (E,1991)
Whitefronted	Russia	6,000–8,000	5,300 (1994)	–
Greylag	Scotland (native)	1,000	5,000 (1995)	–
Brent	Spitsbergen	1,000–3,000	2,100 (1995)	3,000 (1989)
Barnacle	Spitsbergen	400?	13,700 (1995)	–
Bean	Scandinavia/Russia	400?	500 (1995)	–
Total		95,900–102,900	545,050	
Total quarry number		As above	375,300 (including Canadas)	

Note: The WWT co-ordinates all goose counts in the UK and the results are summarised in The Wetland Bird Survey: Wildfowl & Wader Counts.

Index